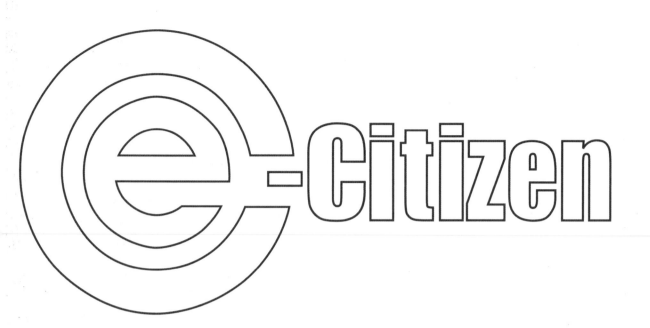

e-citizen

WITHDRAWN

Jenny Lawson

www.heinemann.co.uk

✓ Free online support
✓ Useful weblinks
✓ 24 hour online ordering

01865 888058

Heinemann

Inspiring generations

Heinemann Educational Publishers
Halley Court, Jordan Hill, Oxford OX2 8EJ
Part of Harcourt Education

Heinemann is the registered trademark of Harcourt
Education Limited

© Jenny Lawson, 2006
First published 2006
10 09 08 07 06
10 9 8 7 6 5 4 3 2 1

British Library Cataloguing in Publication Data is available
from the British Library on request.

10-digit ISBN: 0 435 47159 7
13-digit ISBN: 978 0 435471 59 0

Typeset by 𝒯 Tek-Art, Croydon, Surrey
Original illustrations © Harcourt Education Limited, 2006
Printed in Bath Press
Cover photo: © Getty Images
Picture research by Liz Alexander

Acknowledgements
The author and publisher would like to thank the following
individuals and organisations for permission to reproduce
photographs:

iStockphoto/Kerry Garrison p. 4 (top left), Detail
photography/Alamy p. 4 (top right), iStockphoto/Dennys
Bisogno p. 4 (middle), iStockphoto/Kiss Botond p. 4
(bottom), Harcourt Education Ltd/Gareth Bowden p. 7
(top and bottom), iStockphoto/Kian Khoon Tan p. 9 (top),
iStockphoto/Stefan Redel p. 9 (bottom), isifa Image Service
s.r.o./Alamy p. 20 (top left), Eddie Gerald/Alamy p. 20 (top
right), istockphoto/Pederk p. 20 (bottom).

Every effort has been made to contact copyright holders
of material reproduced in this book. Any omissions will be
rectified in subsequent printings if notice is given to the
publishers.

Websites
Please note that the examples of websites suggested
in this book were up to date at the time of writing. It is
essential for tutors to preview each site before using it to
ensure that the URL is still accurate and the content is
appropriate. We suggest that tutors bookmark useful sites
and consider enabling students to access them through the
school or college intranet.

Tel: 01865 888058   www.heinemann.co.uk

European Computer Driving Licence, ECDL, International
Computer Driving Licence, ICDL, e-Citizen and related
logos are trade marks of The European Computer Driving
Licence Foundation Limited ("ECDL-F") in Ireland and other
countries.

Heinemann is an entity independent of ECDL-F and is not
associated with ECDL-F in any manner. This courseware
publication may be used to assist candidates to prepare
for **the e-Citizen test**. Neither ECDL-F nor **Heinemann**
warrants that the use of this courseware publication will
ensure passing of **the e-Citizen test**. This courseware
publication has been independently reviewed and approved
by ECDL-F as complying with the following standard:

*Technical compliance with the learning objectives of e-
Citizen Syllabus Version 1.0.*

Confirmation of this approval can be obtained by reviewing
the Courseware Section of the website www.ecdl.com

The material contained in this courseware publication has
not been reviewed for technical accuracy and does not
guarantee that candidates will pass **the e-Citizen test**.
Any and all assessment items and/or performance-based
exercises contained in this courseware publication relate
solely to this publication and do not constitute or imply
certification by ECDL-F in respect of **the e-Citizen test** or
any other ECDL-F test.

For details on sitting **the e-Citizen test** and other ECDL-F
tests in your country, please contact your country's National
ECDL/ICDL designated Licensee or visit ECDL-F's web site
at www.ecdl.com.

Candidates using this courseware publication must be
registered with the National Licensee, before undertaking
the e-Citizen test. Without a valid registration, **the e-
Citizen test** cannot be undertaken and no **ECDL/ICDL or
e-Citizen** certificate, nor any other form of recognition, can
be given to a candidate. Registration should be undertaken
with your country's National ECDL/ICDL designated
Licensee at any Approved **ECDL/ICDL or e-Citizen** Test
Centre.

e-Citizen Syllabus Version 1.0 is the official syllabus of the
ECDL/ICDL or e-Citizen certification programme at the
date of approval of this courseware publication.

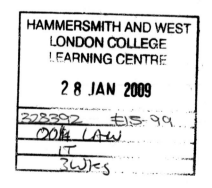

Contents

Introduction

This book is written specifically for those studying for the e-Citizen™ qualification.

The structure of this book

This book is divided into three sections to match the blocks in the specification:

These sections are followed by a Glossary which alphabetically lists all the technical terms used within the text.

An Index is also provided to help you to find what you need within the text.

How to use this book

The material in this book is presented in the order of the syllabus, and this matches the order in which you can study the concepts and practise the skills. So, you can simply start at page 1 and work your way through, learning each skill gradually. For example, you will learn more and more about how to use the Internet as you work through each block:

* In Block 1, you begin to see how the Internet might be useful. You learn some basic definitions and the terminology involved. You look at the Windows Help function, visit some websites and navigate through them.

* In Block 2, you learn how to use a search engine and how to browse to find information on the Internet.

* In Block 3, you develop your skills further so that you can fully participate in facilities offered on the Internet. You learn how to fill in forms online, and look at several different application areas: news, government, consumer, travel, education/training, employment, health, interest groups, and business.

You will also develop skills in using e-mail software:

* In Block 1, you learn the basics: the terminology, how to create a new e-mail message and send it, attaching a file to it, and using an address book. You will also learn how to reply to e-mails and how to forward them.

* In Block 2, you learn about junk mail and how to avoid it, and also how to make use of e-mailing options on a website.

* In Block 3, you use your e-mailing skills to voice your opinion and to request information, e.g. details of a course on which you plan to enrol.

Features of this book

The syllabus is split into topics, with introductory text to each topic giving you some background information and examples as appropriate. Screenshots show you what you might see on your computer screen. There are margin comments too:

What does it mean? are definition of terms that appear in the glossary and are shown in the margin.

Cross reference to other pages help you to find related skills elsewhere in the book.

Remember will jog your memory as to how to do something.

Warning! will remind you of safety issues.

Handy tip will tell you about shortcuts.

DEMO

Demo list things that your tutor will demonstrate or outline in more detail than can be covered in this book.

YOUR TURN!

Your Turn! offer structured exercises that appear at the end of each topic to give you plenty of opportunities for practical experience before you move on to the next topic.

How To... feature provides step-by-step guidelines that explain how to do a specific computer-related task.

In total, this book provides all that you need to cover the entire syllabus of the e-Citizen qualification.

The hardware and software

To complete this course, you will need access to a computer with a printer. You will also need an Internet connection so that you can access the World Wide Web.

The example screenshots are taken from the following standard software in *Windows XP*:

* Microsoft *Word*

* Microsoft *Outlook*.

If you are using earlier or later versions of the same software, your screens may look slightly different. If you are using different software, e.g. a different word processing package, your software will offer much the same options, so you should still be able to work through the book. Also, your tutor will be able to help you.

Acknowledgements

The author and publisher wish to thank all the individuals and organisations who granted permission to reproduce screenshots in the book. Every effort has been made to contact copyright holders of material reproduced in this book. Any omissions will be rectified in subsequent printings if notice is given to the publishers.

Microsoft product screenshot(s) reprinted with permission from Microsoft Corporation

British Airways pp. 16, 146

Crown copyright material reproduced with permission of the Controller of Her Majesty's Stationery Office and the Queen's Printer for Scotland pp. 17, 122, 139, 155, 158, 187, 190, 211, 212

BT Yahoo! pp. 69, 80, 85, 92, 99, 100, 103

Google pp. 70, 101, 102, 149

Stephen Gritton (owner of www.writersdock.co.uk) and authors, Guy Gavriel Kay and Ida Jones pp. 70, 164, 186

Expedia.co.uk pp. 72, 198, 199

Anne Rainbow pp. 74, 108, 109, 110

© 2006 InfoSpace, Inc. All rights reserved. Reprinted with permission of Infospace, Inc. p. 104

Ask.com p. 106

Multimap, Tele Atlas, and Ordnance Survey of the UK p. 114

McAfee p. 121

Friendsreunited.com pp. 125, 175

iwf.org.uk pp. 130, 181

Telegraph Group Limited p. 133

BBC p. 134

FTSE p. 135

Guildford Borough Council p. 138

UK Office of the European Parliament p. 140

Homecrafts Direct p. 141

Sainsbury's Supermarkets Ltd p. 142

Barclays p. 143

thetrainline pp. 147, 177

Surrey County Council pp. 151, 202, 204–206

© 2006 WEA Community Grid for Learning. All rights reserved. p. 152

Leeds University Library p. 153

The National Centre for Complementary and Alternative Medicine p. 160

VSO p. 162

Totaljobs.com p. 172, 209

© 2006 Amazon.com. All rights reserved. pp. 179, 193

Guardian Unlimited p. 185, 207, 215

The Electoral Commission (www.aboutmyvote.co.uk) p. 190

Vauxhall p. 194

Lastminute.com p. 195

National Consumer Federation p. 197

UpMyStreet.com p. 200

Foundation skills

In this block, you will learn the necessary skills and knowledge for essential computer and Internet use.

* You will learn about computer hardware and software.

* You will find out how to handle files and folders.

* You will begin to recognise the icons and other things that you see on your computer screen.

* You will learn how to create a simple document.

* You will browse the Internet to search for information.

* You will learn how to use e-mail to communicate with other computer users.

Lifeskills and benefits from use

When you have completed Block 1 of this course, you should be able to:

* use a personal computer and work with icons, windows and folders
* perform routine Internet-related tasks
* prepare simple documents and text files and print and store them
* connect to the Internet securely and navigate through web pages
* communicate by e-mail without risk.

You will then be ready to tackle the Block 1 questions in the test – and move on to study Blocks 2 and 3.

The computer

In this section, you will learn about your computer: the hardware and software that you will need to be able to use.

You will also learn about your **desktop** – what you will see on the screen – and how you can use your mouse and keyboard to access the features available on your computer.

You will also learn how to turn on – and turn off – your computer safely.

What does it mean?

DESKTOP
Like a real life desktop, what you see onscreen: your documents and tools such as a clock and a calculator.

The hardware bits

Some hardware is essential.

* **Input devices** – like a **keyboard** or **mouse** – let you enter data. Moving the mouse moves the cursor – or pointer – on the screen.
* **Storage devices** – like a hard disk drive – hold the data and serve as extra memory for the computer.
* **Output devices** – like the monitor or screen and your printer – present the data to you as information.

Hard disk drive

A hard disk drive is usually inside the main **processor** box. You cannot see it unless you open up the computer case.

An external hard drive can be attached to a computer, to provide additional storage.

Internal hard drive

External hard drive

Printers

Inkjet printer

There are two main types of printer.

* In an inkjet printer the ink is squirted on to the paper.
* In a laser printer the image is created using toner filings that are glued to the paper using heat. This is similar to the way in which a photocopy is created.

Laser printer

KEYBOARD
See page 22.

MOUSE
See page 20.

What does it mean?

PROCESSOR
The part of the computer that controls all other parts – its 'brain'.

YOUR TURN!

Can you correctly identify all the items of equipment that make up a personal computer in the home or the workplace? Watch the demonstration given by your tutor and then carry out the activities.

1 Look at the following diagrams and name all the items of equipment shown.

DEMO

Your tutor will show you the component parts of a computer.

2 Draw a diagram to show the equipment around your own PC, and label each item.

Turning on your computer

DEMO
Your tutor will show you how to turn on your computer.

It is important that you use the correct procedure to turn on your computer.

HOW TO... **Turn on your computer**

 1 Check the power supply.

 2 Check all connections.

 3 Press the ON switch.

Check the power supply

In the UK, the power supply voltage is 240V. Elsewhere, it is only 110V. Make sure you have the correct setting on your computer.

Check that your computer is plugged into the mains socket, and that the socket switch is turned on.

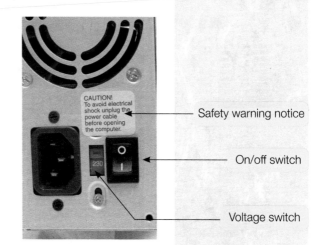

Safety warning notice

On/off switch

Voltage switch

Check all connections

Most peripherals need to be connected to a **port** on the computer, with a lead. Check that there are enough ports for the number of **peripheral** devices you plan to use with your computer.

What does it mean?

PORT
Part of the computer which enables you to connect extra devices.

PERIPHERAL
An input or output device that is attached to a computer, e.g. mouse, keyboard, printer.

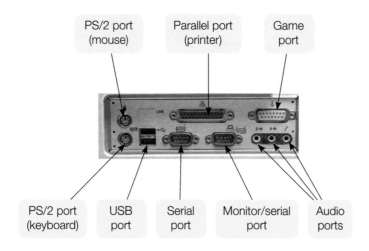

PS/2 port (mouse)   Parallel port (printer)   Game port

PS/2 port (keyboard)   USB port   Serial port   Monitor/serial port   Audio ports

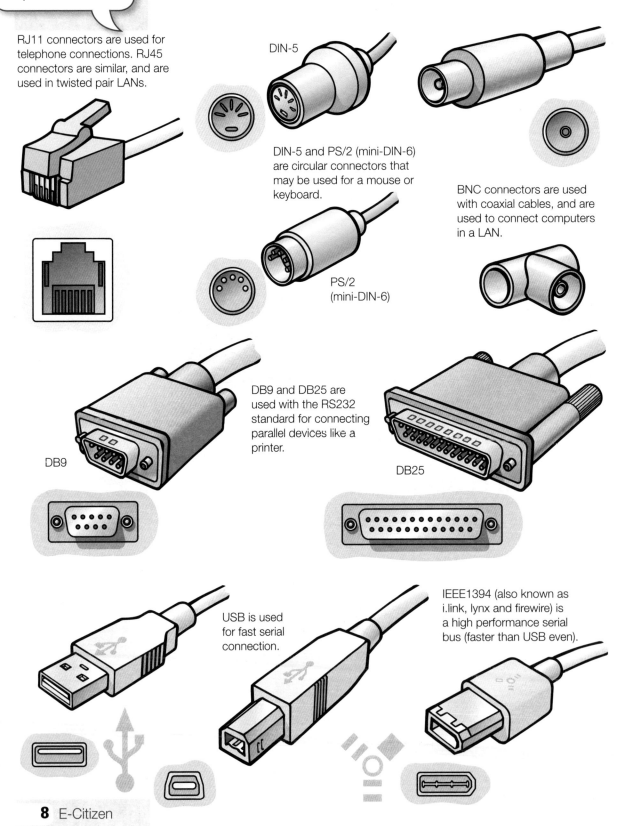

Each lead has a connector that needs to be fitted into the correct
port. There are lots of different types of connector. Make sure that the
connector matches the port to which it is to be connected.

RJ11 connectors are used for
telephone connections. RJ45
connectors are similar, and are
used in twisted pair LANs.

DIN-5

DIN-5 and PS/2 (mini-DIN-6)
are circular connectors that
may be used for a mouse or
keyboard.

PS/2
(mini-DIN-6)

BNC connectors are used
with coaxial cables, and are
used to connect computers
in a LAN.

DB9 and DB25 are
used with the RS232
standard for connecting
parallel devices like a
printer.

DB9

DB25

USB is used
for fast serial
connection.

IEEE1394 (also known as
i.link, lynx and firewire) is
a high performance serial
bus (faster than USB even).

Press the ON switch

Pressing the ON switch should now start your computer. If nothing happens, first check the power supply.

❋ Is the computer connected to the mains supply?

❋ Is it turned on at the wall?

Try again, pressing the ON switch. If still nothing happens, check all the connections. You may be seeing nothing on your screen, just because the screen is not correctly connected.

⚠ WARNING! Make sure it is safe to switch on the power before you flick the switch.

YOUR TURN!

1 Look at your computer and identify the voltage switch. Check that it is set correctly for your power supply.

2 Look at your computer and check all the connections. Make sure every connector is firmly in place.

3 Press the ON switch for your computer.

⚠ WARNING! Make sure you have the correct voltage setting on your computer.

All about icons and menus

ICONS
See page 10.

Icons are used to represent **applications** on the desktop. Icons may also be used to represent other things, like files and folders (page 30).

What does it mean?

APPLICATIONS
The programs that are on your computer, like *Word* and *Excel*.

LEFT-CLICK
See page 20.

DOUBLE-CLICK
See page 20.

Using your mouse to **left-click** on an icon has the effect of selecting the application. **Double-clicking** on an application icon opens the application and starts it running. What you next see is the workspace for that application.

Main menu toolbar

Formatting toolbar

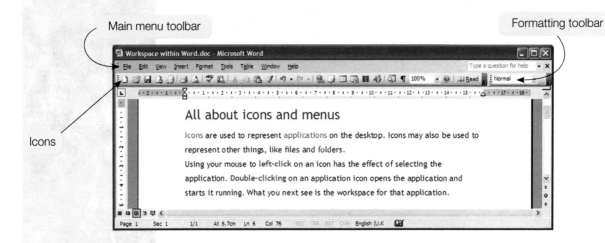

Icons

Around the workspace there are menus and toolbars. On the toolbars, there are lots more icons.

DEMO

Your tutor may show you another way to open an application, using the Start button.

YOUR TURN!

1 Double-click on an application icon, such as the one for *Word*. Study the workspace for that application.

2 Guess what some of the icons mean.

Menus

The commands that you can use are offered on menu bars and on **toolbars**.

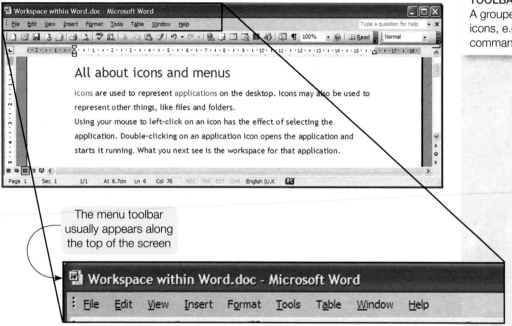

The menu toolbar usually appears along the top of the screen

Other toolbars can offer options for formatting text, or for viewing a document.

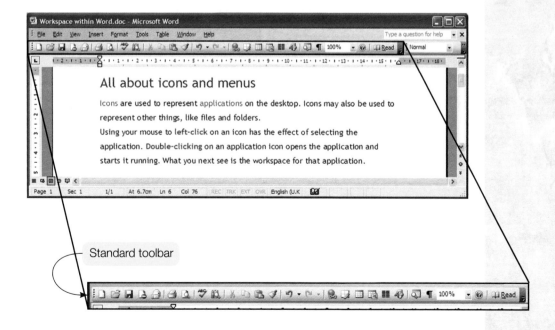

Standard toolbar

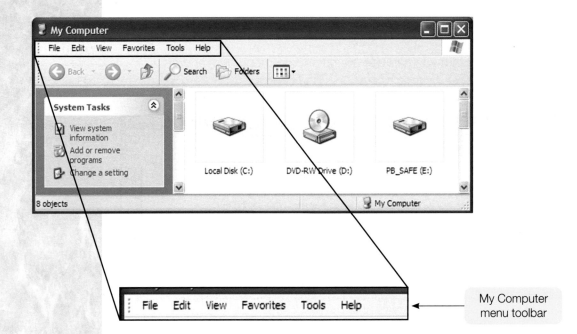

File　Edit　View　Favorites　Tools　Help　◄————　My Computer
menu toolbar

LEFT-CLICK
See page 20.

ROLLING
See page 20.

LEFT-CLICK See page 20.
ROLLING See page 20.

Left-clicking on a menu option, like File or Tools, or **rolling** the cursor over it, will reveal a list of options.

❉ The options are listed in groups, not in alphabetical order.

❉ Some items may be greyed out if they are not available to you right now.

❉ The most frequently used options may appear at the top of the list, rather than in a set position. If so, you will see two arrows ⊻ at the end of the list. To see the full list of options, click on these arrows.

❉ In the left-hand margin of the list, an icon shows that this menu option is also available as a button on a toolbar. Look out for the icon on a toolbar.

❉ In the right-hand margin of the list, an arrowhead indicates that there are further options. Rolling the mouse near the arrow will reveal a submenu of choices.

❉ If a letter is underlined, like the F in File, you can use this single key, with the Alt key, as a **shortcut**.

❉ If the option is followed with a code such as Ctrl-F4, this means there is a **function key** shortcut. Ctrl-F4 is the shortcut for File/Exit.

What does it mean?

SHORTCUT
A key combination or a mouse button that jumps you to an option.

FUNCTION KEYS
The twelve keys along the top of the keyboard.

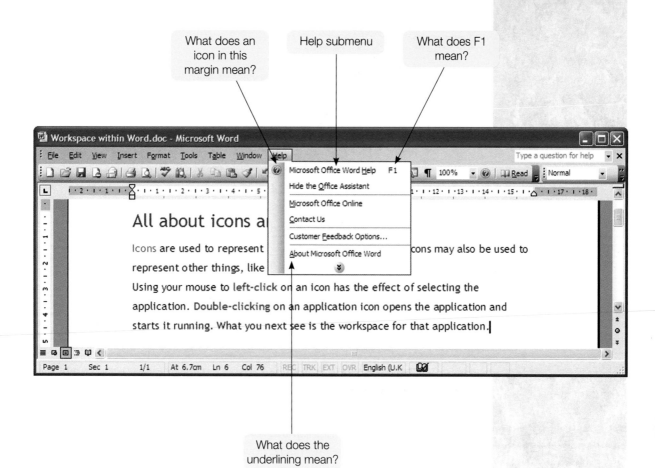

What does an icon in this margin mean?

Help submenu

What does F1 mean?

What does the underlining mean?

YOUR TURN!

1 Left-click on each option in the main menu bar to see what options are listed. Roll the mouse down to view any submenus.

2 Notice the shortcut key options for the function keys. Build up a list of what each of the function keys does: F1, F2 ...

3 Experiment with selecting an option in the main menu bar, using only the letters that are underlined with Alt shift key. Try these in particular: Alt-F, Alt-H.

Icons

An icon is a small picture used to represent something. The best icons are the ones that you recognise easily!

The standard toolbar has icons that are used the most.

FOLDER
See page 31.

BROWSE
See page 39.

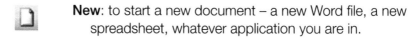 **New**: to start a new document – a new Word file, a new spreadsheet, whatever application you are in.

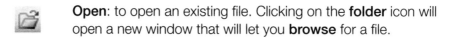 **Open**: to open an existing file. Clicking on the **folder** icon will open a new window that will let you **browse** for a file.

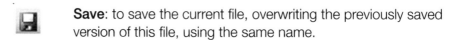 **Save**: to save the current file, overwriting the previously saved version of this file, using the same name.

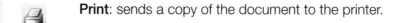 **Print**: sends a copy of the document to the printer.

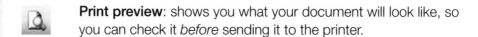 **Print preview**: shows you what your document will look like, so you can check it *before* sending it to the printer.

What does it mean?

CLIPBOARD
A temporary place for things when you cut or copy them; see page 38.

 **Cut:** cuts the highlighted text and places it on the **clipboard**. The highlighted text is removed.

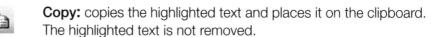 **Copy:** copies the highlighted text and places it on the clipboard. The highlighted text is not removed.

 **Paste:** inserts the contents of the clipboard at the current cursor position. It will replace any highlighted text.

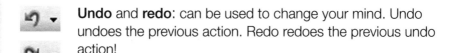 **Undo** and **redo**: can be used to change your mind. Undo undoes the previous action. Redo redoes the previous undo action!

These icons are common to many applications. For example, applications produced by *Microsoft*, such as *Word* and *Excel*, use the same icon for the same command, like printing and saving. This makes it easier to learn to use a new application; you will find that you recognise the workspace very quickly.

There are also icons on the desktop for other applications. The icon in the margin is for Internet Explorer, which will connect you to the Internet.

When you are accessing the Internet, whatever software you use will have standard browser icons for the commonest of their commands. You will learn about these on page 75.

Internet Explorer

Back   Forward   Stop   Refresh

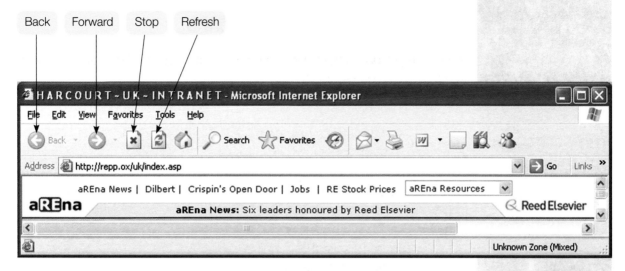

On your desktop, you might also see icons for **My Computer** and **My Documents**.

❋ Clicking on the My Computer icon opens a window which shows the hardware on your computer, such as the different drives.

❋ The My Documents icon takes you to where you store all your work.

One particularly important icon on the desktop is used to represent the **Recycle Bin**. When you **delete** a file, the file appears in a list in the Recycle Bin. It stays there, and can be recovered if you change your mind, until you empty the Recycle Bin.

Emptying the Recycle Bin needs to be done regularly. Otherwise, you could run out of space on your hard drive.

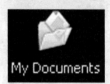

YOUR TURN!

1 Look carefully at the computer screen. Which toolbars are open? To find out, select View/Toolbars.

2 Make sure the Standard toolbar is visible. Identify each icon. If you are not sure, move the cursor near the icon, and find out what it does.

3 Make sure the Formatting toolbar is visible, and identify each icon on it.

4 Working with a friend, test each other to see how many icons you recognise.

5 Use Alt-F4 to close your application, and identify the Recycle Bin on your desktop.

DELETING
See page 42.

DEMO

Your tutor will show how to make a toolbar visible.

! HANDY TIP

You can select – or choose from a menu – by left-clicking on the option.

The computer **15**

What does it mean?

WINDOW
A rectangular area through which you view your workspace.

DESKTOP
See page 3.

All about windows

Microsoft Windows is so called because, on your monitor screen, you look at your work on the **desktop** through windows.

When you double-click on the icon for an application, it opens in a window. This window is then the **active window**. You can have more than one window open, but only one of them is active at any one time. To make a window active, you must click on it; see how it changes. (The panel at the top of the active window may be a darker shade of blue.)

Active window

The Start button can be used to reveal the applications available (see page 17).

The Task bar shows which applications are open.

You can control what you see on your desktop workspace.

* You can have more than one window open at a time. So, for example, you can work on a document such as a letter and look at a spreadsheet at the same time.

* You can lay windows one on top of another, much like you might put things on top of each other on your desk. You can only see what is at the top of the pile.

* You can minimise a window. This is like tucking the work away in a drawer. The application is not closed.

* You can change the size of a window, so that you can fit more than one window on the screen at a time.

* You can move the windows around, so that they are positioned where you want them.

* When you have finished working on an application you can close the window completely. This shuts down that application.

Minimise/Maximise/Restore/Close

In the top right-hand part of each window, three buttons let you control that window:

  You can minimise the window. This results in the window name appearing in the Task bar at the bottom of your desktop. Clicking on it in the Task bar opens the window again. You can **toggle** between full screen (maximise) and part screen (restore down).

 Using only part of the screen for one window will allow you to have more than one window open at a time.

 You can close the window – this generally shuts down the application too.

What does it mean?

TOGGLE
To switch between two states by pressing the same button.

Having more than one window open at a time

If you need to work on two things at the same time, you will need a window open for each.

Having opened one application, minimise that window by clicking on the Minimise button. The application does not close. It is tucked away on your Task bar.

You can then **double-click** on a second application, or use the Start menu to locate the application or document you want to use.

DOUBLE-CLICK
See page 20.

These applications are 'pinned' to the Start menu.

These are the applications you have used recently – you might decide to pin these to the Start menu if you use them a lot.

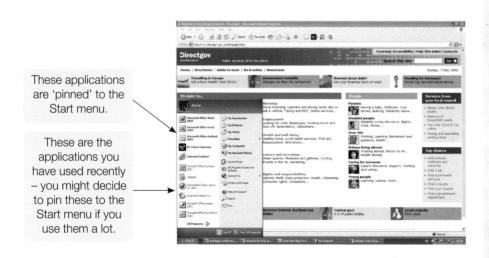

Moving windows: using drag and drop

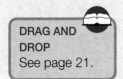

DRAG AND DROP
See page 21.

If you have more than one window open, you may want to move them around on your desktop. However, you can only move an active window.

You can fill your desktop with as many windows as you wish.

Outlook offers a calendar feature which could replace your desk diary.

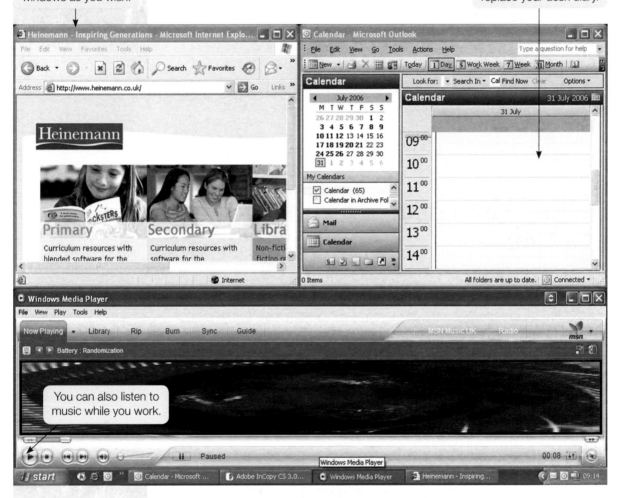

You can also listen to music while you work.

HOW TO... Adjust window position

LEFT-CLICK
See page 20.

☑ 1 Left-click on a window (or, if it has been minimised, click on its title in the Task bar) to make it the active window. The panel at the top of the window goes a darker blue than any of the other windows on the screen.

☑ 2 Move the cursor to the darker blue area of the active window.

☑ 3 Left-click and, holding the mouse button down, drag the cursor until the window is where you want it.

Adjusting window size: using grab handles

HOW TO... Change the size of a window

 1 Position the cursor at a corner – or a side – of the active window, until you see the cursor change to a grab handle.

 2 Left-click the mouse and drag the cursor to where you want that corner or edge to be.

YOUR TURN!

1 Turn on your computer.
2 On the desktop, open the *Microsoft Word* application.
3 Minimise the window so that it appears only in the Task bar.
4 Press the Start button, and select another application, such as *Microsoft Excel*.
5 Click on the Restore Down button so that the new application does not fill the screen.
6 Click on Word in the Task bar. Notice that its window fills the screen, so you cannot see the second application underneath.
7 Click on Restore Down. Resize and move the window so that it takes up the right-hand half of your screen.
8 Click on the second application window to make it active. Resize this window so you can see both windows without any overlap between them.
9 Close the second application window.
10 Click on the Maximise button on the *Word* window to make it fill the screen.
11 Close the *Word* application.

> **REMEMBER**
> Double-clicking on an application icon opens the application.

Using the mouse and keyboard

Every instruction you give to your computer can be made using the mouse – or using the keyboard.

The mouse

Moving the mouse across the desk rolls the cursor over objects on the screen, such as icons. For some icons, this will reveal a message saying what the icon does.

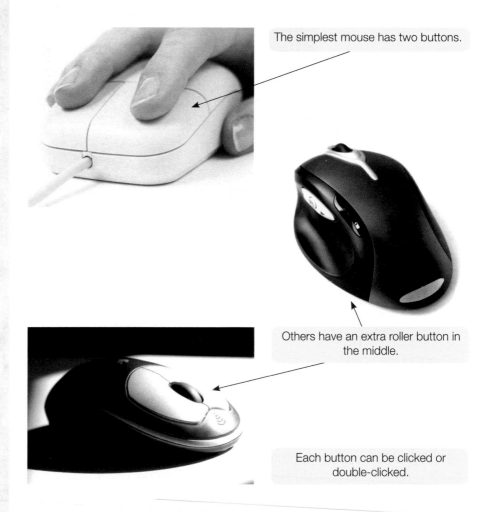

The simplest mouse has two buttons.

Others have an extra roller button in the middle.

Each button can be clicked or double-clicked.

Left-clicking

A mouse can be reprogrammed for left-handed users, so that the actions of each button is reversed. However, usually:

❊ **single left-clicking** (i.e. click and release the button) is used to select an **object** on the screen

❊ **double left-clicking** (two quick clicks and then release) can be used to open applications.

Drag and drop

Drag and drop is used to move objects.

> **HOW TO...** **Drag and drop**
>
> 1 Left-click on the object to select it, but don't release the button.
>
> 2 Slide – or drag – the mouse so that the object moves to a new position.
>
> 3 Release the button to 'drop' whatever you had selected.

Right-clicking

Clicking on the right-hand button (or the left-hand one if your mouse is set up for a left-handed user!) will reveal a context-sensitive menu.

This menu of options will match the actions you might want to do, considering where your cursor was when you right-clicked. This is a useful shortcut to actions.

> The options offered are relevant to the application and to the position of your cursor.

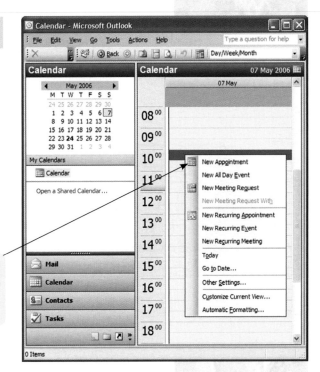

YOUR TURN!

1 Open an application such as *Word*. Practise moving the cursor around the screen by moving the mouse in different directions. Watch to see if the cursor image changes.

2 Roll the cursor over some of the icons to check what they represent.

3 Practise single- and double-clicking using your index finger on the left mouse button.

4 See what options you are offered when you right-click in different areas on the screen.

> **! HANDY TIP**
> Single-clicking has an effect on all icons. Double-clicking only has a different effect on some icons – like application icons.

The keyboard

The keyboard is used to enter data, and also to give commands. The keyboard has many sections!

✳ The QWERTY keyboard includes a **Space bar**, and the **Enter key**.

✳ The number pad includes mathematical keys such as + and a decimal point.

✳ The **Cursor arrow keys** and **Directional keys** let you move the cursor around the screen.

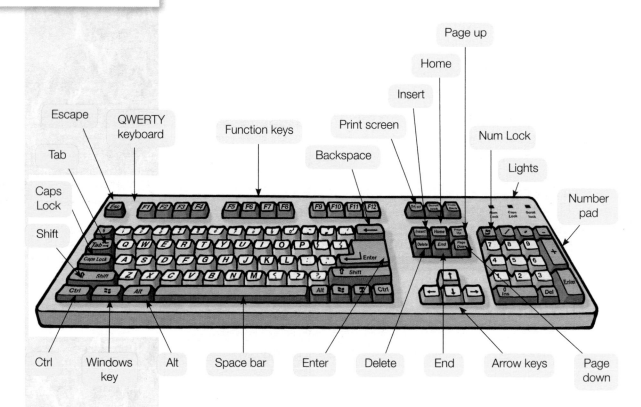

Shift/Caps Lock

The alphabet keys (A–Z) are arranged in the QWERTY layout. Pressing a letter on its own gives a lower case letter.

✳ Holding the Shift key down while pressing a letter changes the 'shift' and makes that letter upper case.

✳ Pressing the Caps Lock key turns all the QWERTY keys into capitals. Pressing Caps Lock again toggles you back to lower case typing. Pressing it again toggles you back to all capitals again, and so on.

Escape/Backspace/Delete

Some keys can get you out of trouble!

❋ The **Escape key** can be used to cancel a command. It clears the current choice so you can choose again.

❋ The **Backspace key** will delete the character to the left of the cursor.

❋ The **Delete key** will delete the character to the right of the cursor.

Tab key

The Tab key jumps the cursor to the next tab stop.

In text, you can set tab stops at particular places, to create a tabulated effect, with the data in columns.

DEMO

Your tutor will show you how to set/clear tab stops.

Function keys

Along the top of the keyboard are the functions keys: F1, F2, F3 ... F12.

Each of these keys has a specific function if pressed alone.

If pressed with the Alt key depressed (or the Ctrl key, or the Shift key) these functions may have other effects.

Alt/Ctrl/Shift

The Alt, Ctrl and Shift keys can be used in combination with other keys, not just the function keys, to create **hot keys**.

What does it mean?

HOT KEYS
Combinations of keys that, when pressed together, have a special effect.

YOUR TURN!

1 Examine a keyboard and check that you know what every key does.

2 Locate the special keys: Enter, Space bar, Shift, Caps Lock, Backspace, Delete, Tab and the arrow keys.

3 Look at a second keyboard with a different layout. Locate all the keys again.

4 Open *Word*. Experiment with typing upper and lower case letters. Use the Space bar, the Backspace and the Delete key, the Tab key and the Enter key.

Shutting down properly

Turning off your computer is not as simple as turning off one switch. You cannot just turn off the power.

You must follow correct procedures. Otherwise, when you next turn on the computer, you will have to wait while the computer checks everything is okay.

HOW TO... Shut down properly

1 Close all applications (see below).

2 Hang up – or disconnect – any dial-up links to the Internet.

3 On the Start menu, select Turn Off Computer

4 Wait for the final menu, and select Turn Off

5 Wait until the screen goes blank, and then switch off all power switches.

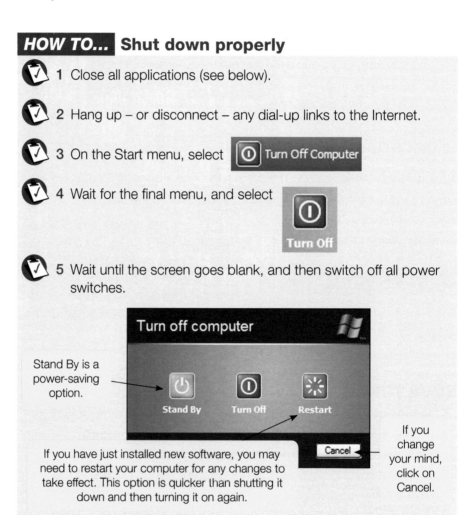

Stand By is a power-saving option.

If you have just installed new software, you may need to restart your computer for any changes to take effect. This option is quicker than shutting it down and then turning it on again.

If you change your mind, click on Cancel.

Closing an application

REMEMBER
You can close an application by clicking on the Close button in the top right-hand corner.

There are three ways you can close an application:

* Click on ☒ in the top right-hand corner.
* Select File/Exit on the Main menu bar.
* Use the shortcut: Alt-F4.

However, you should save your work first, and might want to close the document without closing an application. There are two ways to do this:

* Select File/Close on the Main menu toolbar.
* Use the shortcut: Ctrl-F4.

If you close the application and have forgotten to save your work, you will be warned. You will be offered the option to Cancel the close, or to Save your work, or not to bother saving! Think carefully before closing an application without saving your work. If you do, any changes you made since the last time you saved your work will be lost.

SAVING
See page 59.

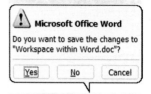

Microsoft Office Word

Do you want to save the changes to "Workspace within Word.doc"?

| Yes | No | Cancel |

DEMO

Your tutor will show you how to recover from a power failure problem.

YOUR TURN!

1 Turn on your computer and open several applications.
2 Turn off your computer, following correct procedure.

Using Help

No matter how experienced you become on a computer – or how new you are! – you will need help sometimes.

Help is available in different forms:

* You could ask a friend, or your teacher, to show you how to do something.
* You could read a book like this one, or a manual.
* You could use the **online help**.

What does it mean?

ONLINE HELP
Guidance about an application, built into the software or available over the Internet.

The Help function key: F1

Pressing F1 will open up the Help function for the application you are using. Or you can select Help from the main menu toolbar.

(Alt-H opens this drop-down menu automatically – try it!)

See page 29 for the Word Help menu options. Notice how the options on the Help menus are similar for all applications.

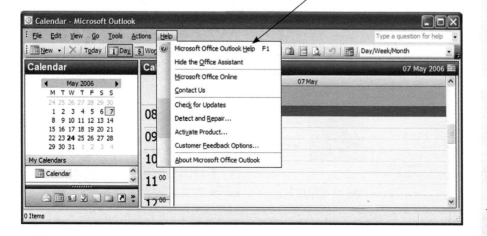

What does it mean?

DEFAULT
A setting that is decided by the software vendor, but one that you can change if you want.

The Office Assistant

In some applications, such as *Word*, there is an Office Assistant, that pops up when you open the application.

The **default** Assistant is Clippit the paperclip, but you can choose a different one from a collection of others, like Links the cat here.

Internet Help

If you cannot find what you need from the Help files available with the application you are working on, all is not lost.

If you have a link to the Internet, you can look for help directly from the manufacturer of your software.

You could connect, for example, to the *Microsoft* Office Online Help option.

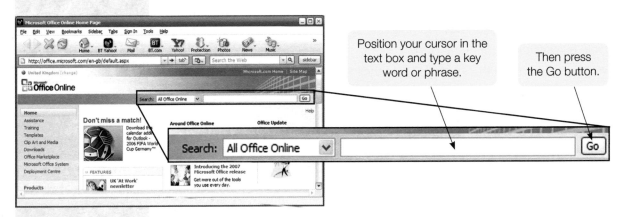

Position your cursor in the text box and type a key word or phrase.

Then press the Go button.

What does it mean?

SEARCH KEY
The keywords needed to find what you are looking for.

Keyword search option

Whichever source of help you decide on, if it is electronic, you will need to enter a **search key**. The figure below shows a search for 'office assistant'.

When you click on Search, the search results are presented as a list of topics. Each item is a **hotlink** to a help file. If you click on the link, the help page is displayed.

The help information appears in a separate panel, called a Task pane, so you can read it and follow the instructions at the same time.

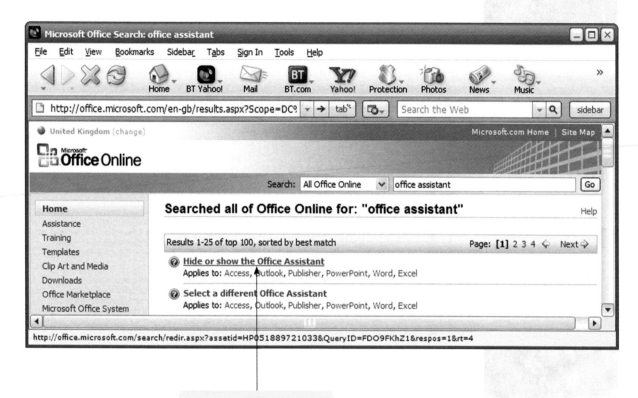

Click on a hotlink to reveal the help that you need.

YOUR TURN!

1 Turn on your computer and open up *Word* or another word processing package. Spend five minutes typing some words describing the weather today.

2 Select Help from the main menu and make sure the Office Assistant is not hidden.

3 In the Search box, type the search key: 'word count'.

4 Click on Search (or a green right arrow if there is one) to start the search.

5 Click on the Help list item to find out how to count the words in your document.

6 Follow the instructions. How many words did you type?

The Contents option

In some applications, like *Internet Explorer*, the help files that are displayed when you do a search are also available using the Contents option.

Click on Help in Internet Explorer and select 'Contents and Index'. This window will open.

Select the section and subsection that interests you ...

... and relevant helpful notes will appear, explaining how to achieve what you want.

Click on a hotlink for more information.

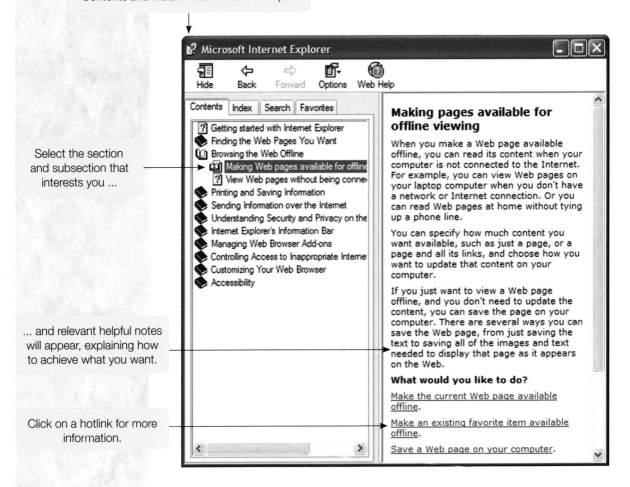

If you click on an item in the Contents list, that section opens up to reveal subsections. Some subsections will then open into even greater detail.

YOUR TURN!

1 Turn on your computer and open *Internet Explorer*, or some other browser.
2 Use the Contents option to search for information on how to make web pages available for offline viewing.

The Index option

In much the same way that a book might have an index, the help files are also indexed. If you 'look up' a word, each 'page' that word appears on, in a Help file, can be displayed.

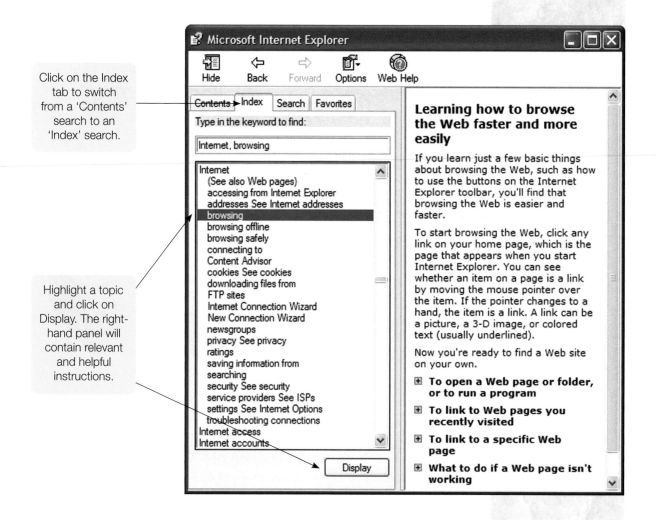

Click on the Index tab to switch from a 'Contents' search to an 'Index' search.

Highlight a topic and click on Display. The right-hand panel will contain relevant and helpful instructions.

YOUR TURN!

1 Turn on your computer and open another application such as *Word*.
2 Experiment with locating help in various ways: using the F1 key, using the Help option on the main menu, etc.
3 In *Word*, use the Office Assistant to find out how to create a new document, and how to save it.
4 Use the Index search to find out how to change the orientation of a printed web page to landscape.

Files and folders

In this section, you will learn about how to find your work on your computer, and to manage the storage of your files and folders.

Viewing folders

Each piece of work – each document or spreadsheet or database – is stored in a file, and these files are stored in folders (or **directories**).

Directory structure

All your document files are stored on your computer in the My Documents folder.

HOW TO... **View files**

1 Use your mouse to click on Start to reveal the Start menu. Or press the Start button on your keyboard.

2 Left-click on My Documents.

What does it mean?

DIRECTORY
Pre-Windows name for a folder – where files are stored.

REMEMBER
Page 22 shows how the keyboard is laid out.

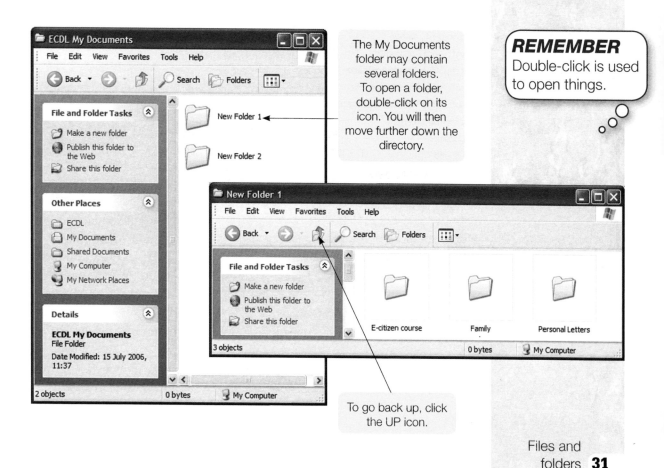

The My Documents folder may contain several folders. To open a folder, double-click on its icon. You will then move further down the directory.

REMEMBER
Double-click is used to open things.

To go back up, click the UP icon.

Creating a new folder

If you set up different folders for different areas of your work, you will be able to find things again more easily.

HOW TO... Create a new folder

 1 Open the folder in which you want to create a new folder, e.g. My Documents.

 2 Select File/New/Folder from the main menu.

> File/New is an option on most main menu toolbars. You are then offered whatever is relevant for the application.

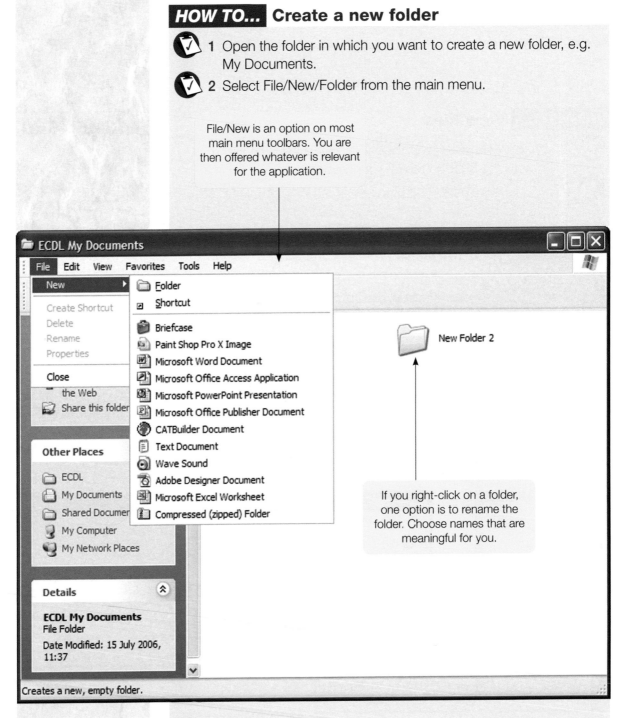

> If you right-click on a folder, one option is to rename the folder. Choose names that are meaningful for you.

 3 A new folder icon is created. Type in the name you want to use.

Directory view

The amount of information shown for each file, and the way this is presented, depends on what you choose for the Views option. There are five options, some of which are illustrated on these pages:

- Thumbnails
- Tiles
- Icons
- List
- Details

For image files, there is also the option of a filmstrip.

ICONS
See page 13.

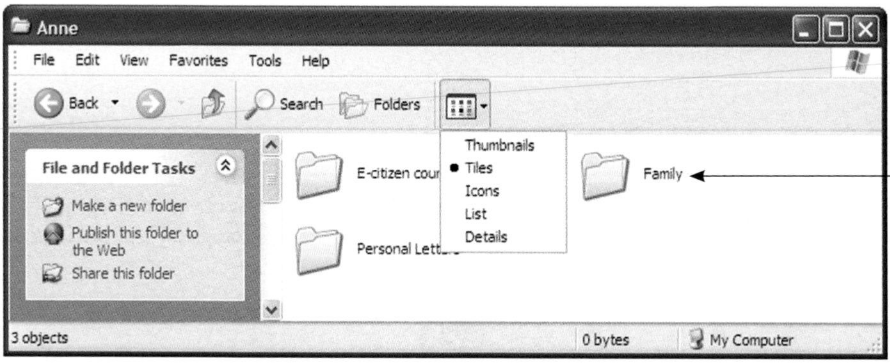

These files are shown using Tile view ...

... but the Details option presents the information as a list.

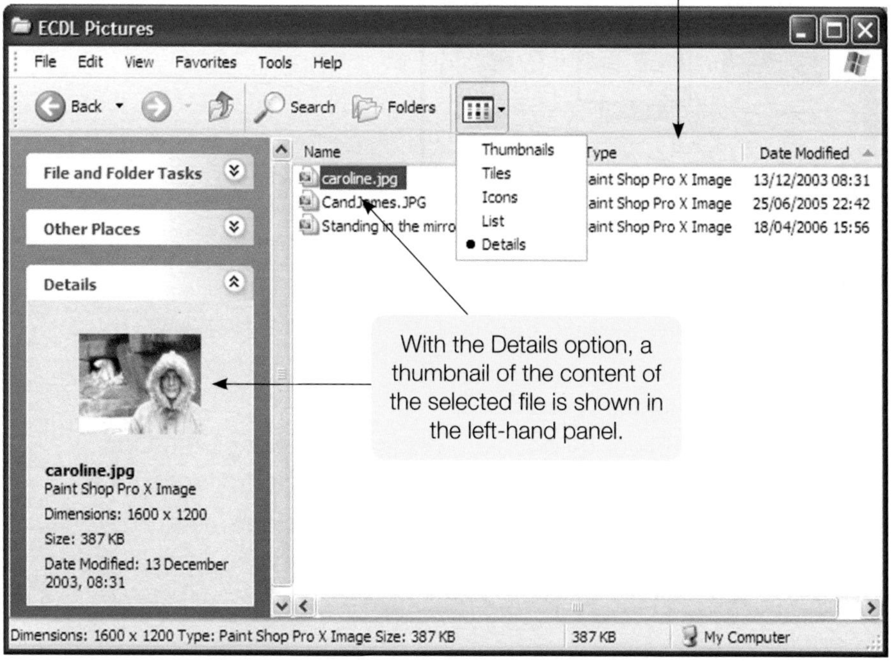

With the Details option, a thumbnail of the content of the selected file is shown in the left-hand panel.

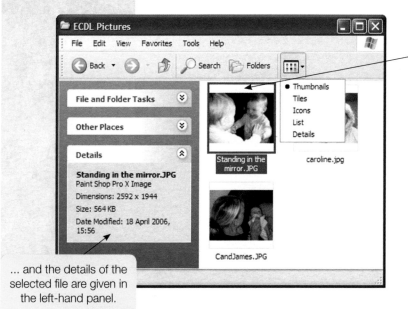

With Thumbnails view, the content of each file is shown in the right-hand panel ...

... and the details of the selected file are given in the left-hand panel.

The Filmstrip option is available within the My Pictures folder. Placing your pictures there provides an easy way to view your photos.

YOUR TURN!

1 Use your mouse to open the Start menu. Left-click on My Documents.

2 Create a new folder called ECDL.

3 Open another folder by double-clicking on it. Change the View option to confirm what thumbnails and tiles look like for your files.

4 Using the keyboard, not the mouse, open the Start menu and select the My Pictures folder.

5 Experiment with the Views option to see how Icon, List, Details and Filmstrip look.

File types

Because there are different types of information to be stored on a computer – characters, numbers, images – and different software applications – word processors, spreadsheets, databases – that create and process this information, there are many different types of files:

❋ text files

❋ word processing files

❋ web page files

❋ image files.

Tiles

If you choose to view your files as tiles, the image used for each file indicates the application used to create the file, and the file type.

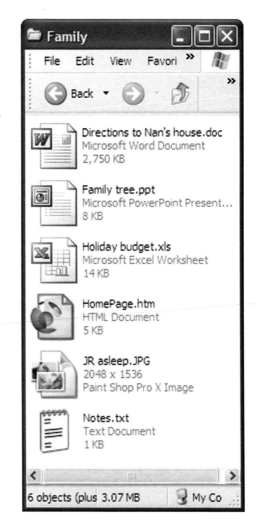

File extensions

When you save your work, you choose a filename for it, but you also decide the type of file, **and** this is stored as part of the name – as the **file extension** (see the table below).

File type	Common file extensions
Text files	RTF or TXT
Documents	DOC or WPS
Web page files	HTM or HTML
Images	JPG or TIF or BMP

SAVING
See page 59.

What does it mean?

FILE EXTENSION
A 3- or 4-character code that appears after the dot in a filename.

Hiding/showing extensions

It is possible to opt to hide file extensions, although you are advised not to do this.

HOW TO... Hide/reveal file extensions

 1 Open the Start menu, and select My Documents.

 2 On the main menu, select Tools/Folder Options.

 3 Click on the View tab.

 4 Make sure that the box marked 'Hide extensions for known file types' has not been ticked.

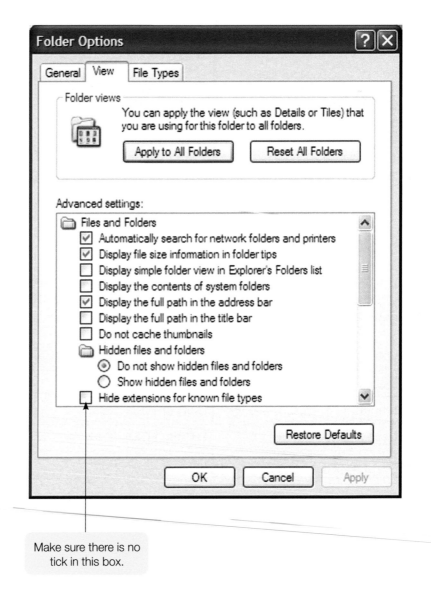

Make sure there is no tick in this box.

Grouping files by format

If you use the Details option to view your files, the file type is shown in one column.

 HOW TO... **Group files by format**

1 View your files using the Details option.

 2 Click on the column heading 'Type' to sort the files according to their file type.

 3 Click again to reverse the order.

Click on the arrowhead to reverse the order.

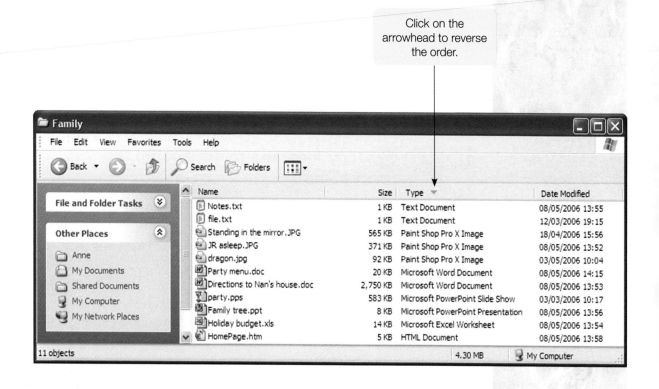

Name	Size	Type ▽	Date Modified
Notes.txt	1 KB	Text Document	08/05/2006 13:55
file.txt	1 KB	Text Document	12/03/2006 19:15
Standing in the mirror.JPG	565 KB	Paint Shop Pro X Image	18/04/2006 15:56
JR asleep.JPG	371 KB	Paint Shop Pro X Image	08/05/2006 13:52
dragon.jpg	92 KB	Paint Shop Pro X Image	03/05/2006 10:04
Party menu.doc	20 KB	Microsoft Word Document	08/05/2006 14:15
Directions to Nan's house.doc	2,750 KB	Microsoft Word Document	08/05/2006 13:53
party.pps	583 KB	Microsoft PowerPoint Slide Show	03/03/2006 10:17
Family tree.ppt	8 KB	Microsoft PowerPoint Presentation	08/05/2006 13:56
Holiday budget.xls	14 KB	Microsoft Excel Worksheet	08/05/2006 13:54
HomePage.htm	5 KB	HTML Document	08/05/2006 13:58

11 objects   4.30 MB   My Computer

YOUR TURN!

1 Open the Start menu and select My Documents. Change the Views option to Tiles. Study the various designs of tile and identify the file types.

2 Choose the Details option and experiment with clicking on the column headings to see how you can reorder the files, e.g. by filename or by date created.

Copying files and folders

DRAG AND DROP
See page 21.

There are two ways of copying files (and folders) from one place in your directory structure to another place:

❋ by copying the file on to the clipboard, and then pasting it into place

❋ using the File and Folder Tasks panel.

If you want to copy files or folders from one media to another you can also use **drag and drop**.

Using the clipboard to copy files and folders

The clipboard is a temporary store that can be used to move things from one place to another. It can be used to move objects from one folder to another, or from one drive to another. You can move text, images, cells from a spreadsheet, records from a database, and files and folders.

You can also use the clipboard to move things from one application workspace to the workspace of another application, e.g. from a web page to a *Word* document, from a spreadsheet to a *Word* document, or from a *Word* document into a *PowerPoint* slideshow.

HOW TO... **Copy files and folders using the clipboard**

 1 Select the object that you want to copy, to highlight it.

 2 Copy the object to the clipboard using one of the three ways shown in the table below.

 3 Move the cursor to the destination point. This can be a different folder or a different drive. Select the drive from My Computer. Within a drive, move down the directory by double-clicking on a folder name and move up by clicking on the UP icon.

 4 Paste the contents of the clipboard to this new place (see the table again for the options).

DEMO
Your tutor will show you how to locate your destination point.

Copying options	Pasting options
Choose Edit on the main menu and select Copy.	Choose Edit on the main menu and select Paste.
Right-click and select Copy from the context-sensitive menu.	Right-click and select Paste from the context-sensitive menu.
Use the shortcut key: Ctrl-C	Use the shortcut key: Ctrl-V

You can choose any combination of these copy and paste options – whichever method you find easiest.

Using the File and Folder Tasks panel

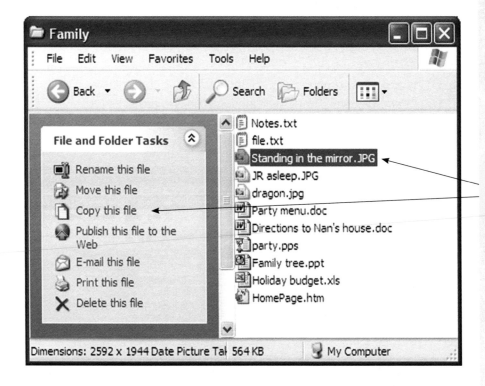

Select a file to reveal the complete list of file and folder tasks.

REMEMBER
Single-click is used to select objects.

HOW TO... Copy files and folders using the File and Folder Tasks panel

 1 Locate the source file or folder through My Computer or My Documents. Select whatever you want to copy.

 2 Click on 'Copy this file' on the File and Folder Tasks panel.

 3 As directed, **browse** for where the file or folder is to be pasted.

What does it mean?

BROWSE
To click your way through your directory structure until you find a particular file or folder.

Copying from one media to another

To copy a file or folder from one media to another, you can use either of the two methods already seen:

❋ Copy/paste using the clipboard, or using the File and Folder Tasks panel.

❋ Use drag and drop (usually used to move files and folders).

Copying more than one file/folder at a time

When selecting the source file/folder, you can select more than one.

❋ Having selected one, hold the Ctrl key down and select any others that you want to copy at the same time. (You can also deselect files and folders this way.)

❋ Or, having selected one file or folder, hold down the Shift key. When you next click, every file/folder between the two are selected.

Notice how the list of file and folder tasks changes when you select a second file.

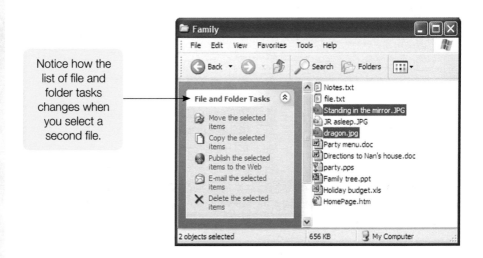

YOUR TURN!

1 In My Documents, you should have a folder called ECDL. Browse My Computer to locate this folder.

2 In a separate window, browse to locate the My Pictures folder. Copy one of the sample pictures to the ECDL folder.

3 Experiment with copying more files/folders, more than one at a time.

4 Experiment with copying files and folders between different media.

REMEMBER
You can sort files into a specific order; see page 37.

! HANDY TIP
When you copy or cut, something is written to the clipboard. Paste uses the last thing you cut/copied, unless you select another item on the clipboard.

Moving files and folders

Moving files/folders is very similar to copying them, except the original file is no longer where it was.

❋ The File and Folder Tasks panel offers all the options you might need: copy or move. When you select an option, it then guides you, step by step, to complete the task successfully.

❋ You can also use the clipboard. Instead of copy and paste, you can cut and paste.

Using drag and drop to move files and folders

To use drag and drop, you must have two windows open:

✳ the source folder, where the file/folder is now

✳ the destination folder, where you want the file/folder to be moved to.

You can then drag the file/folder from one to the other.

HOW TO... **Move a file/folder**

 1 Go to My Documents. Click on folders until the source window is open and you can see the file/folder that you want to move. Change the size of this window so that you can fit a second window on your screen.

ADJUSTING WINDOW SIZE See page 19.

 2 Click on Start and go to My Documents again. Locate the destination folder. Resize this window so that you can see both windows at once.

 3 Click on the source file/folder so that it is highlighted. Without releasing the mouse button, drag the file/folder to the other window, and then release the mouse button to drop the file/folder there.

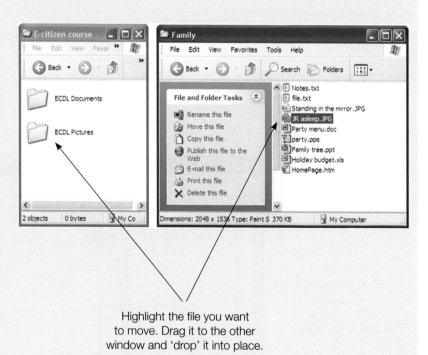

Highlight the file you want to move. Drag it to the other window and 'drop' it into place.

 4 The file/folder will be moved automatically.

What does it mean?

LOGICAL DRIVE
A disk drive is given a logical drive letter: A and B for floppy disks, C for the hard drive, D for a CD, and so on.

You can also use drag and drop to move material from your hard drive (**logical drive** C:) to a CD (maybe on drive D:) and vice versa.

From the Start menu, instead of going to My Documents, go to My Computer and select the device for your source and/or destination folders.

YOUR TURN!

1 Create a new folder within the ECDL folder and call it ECDL Pictures. Browse to locate the image file in your ECDL folder. Move this image file to the ECDL Pictures folder.

2 Insert a CD into your CD drive and view the files on it. Copy all the files from the CD to the My Documents folder. Create a new folder in your ECDL folder using a name that matches the contents of the CD. Move all the files from My Documents into your new folder.

3 Experiment with using other options on the File and Folder Tasks panel.

What does it mean?

HOUSEKEEPING
Keeping the storage space tidy, often by deleting unwanted files and folders.

Deleting files and folders

Part of the **housekeeping** of a computer is to delete files and folders that are no longer needed.

If you never delete any files, you could eventually run out of disk storage space.

As with Copy/Cut/Paste, there are several ways of deleting a file or folder once you have selected it:

Having highlighted a file, you can delete it using the File and Folder Task panel ...

... or right-click to reveal the context-sensitive menu and choose Delete.

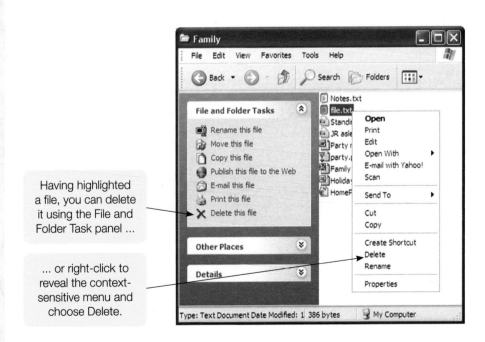

❊ You could choose Edit on the main menu and select Delete.

❊ You could right-click and select Delete from the context-sensitive menu.

The File and Folder Tasks panel also offers an option to delete a file or folder.

The Recycle Bin

When you delete a file, it is placed in the Recycle Bin. It is not deleted completely until you empty the Recycle Bin. So, you still have the option to restore a file or folder if you change your mind, until you empty the bin.

What does it mean?

RECYCLE BIN
A folder that holds all the deleted files and folders until you empty it.

HOW TO... **Restore a deleted file from the Recycle Bin**

 1 Locate, in the Recycle Bin, the deleted file that you want to restore. You may need to browse through folders if it was in a folder that you deleted.

 2 Select the file by clicking on it.

 3 Right-click and select Restore; or select Restore this file from the Recycle Bin Tasks panel.

 4 The file/folder disappears from view, but will be back in its original location, prior to your deleting it.

HOW TO... **Empty the Recycle Bin**

 1 From the Desktop, double-click on the Recycle Bin to open it.

 2 Make sure there is nothing you might want to restore.

 3 Click on Empty the Recycle Bin in the Recycle Bin Tasks panel.

 4 A warning message is displayed. Only click Yes if you are absolutely sure you want to delete the files in your Recycle Bin permanently. Once you click Yes, the files will be lost forever.

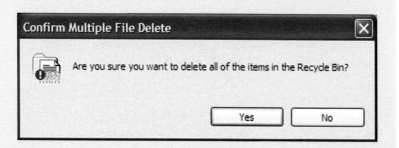

Confirm Multiple File Delete

Are you sure you want to delete all of the items in the Recycle Bin?

Yes   No

YOUR TURN!

1 View the contents of your Recycle Bin; it is on your desktop.

2 Delete a file – and then restore it.

3 Check that there is nothing in the Recycle Bin that you might want to restore. Restore anything you want to keep and then empty the Recycle Bin.

Simple applications

In this section, you will learn about simple applications.

What does it mean?

TEXT EDITOR
Software that offers simple but very limited features to create a text file.

WORD PROCESSING PACKAGE
Sophisticated software that offers more features than a text editor.

Creating a new document

Documents can be created using a **text editor** such as *Notepad*, or a **word processing package** such as *Word*.

Using Notepad

Notepad is located in the *Accessories* folder.

HOW TO... **Open Notepad**

 1 Click on Start and select All Programs.

 2 Point to the Accessories folder.

 3 Select Notepad.

What does it mean?

WORDWRAP
Formatting option which automatically puts text on to a new line when a line is filled.

YOUR TURN!

1 Open *Notepad* and write a few lines about yourself, without pressing Enter.

2 Select Format and click on **Wordwrap** to turn it off. See what happens to the text. Increase the width of the window to view more of the text if necessary.

3 Switch Wordwrap back on.

Opening a new document

Whichever application you are using, the method of opening a new file is the same.

NEW ICON
See page 14.

HOW TO... Open a new document

 1 Open the application: *Word* or some other word processing package.

 2 On the main menu toolbar, select File/New. This opens a dialogue box in which you should select Blank Document. Or, click on the **New icon** on the Standard toolbar. Or, use the keyboard shortcut: Ctrl-N. (These last two options automatically open a blank document.)

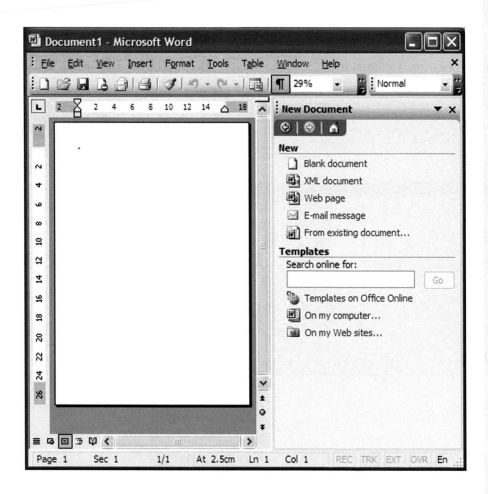

YOUR TURN!

1 Open *Word* or another word processing package and create three new documents, each by using a different method.

Opening existing documents

One of the benefits of using a computer to write letters, reports and other documents is the option to start work on a document one day, and then carry on developing it at a later date.

To do this, you need to follow a development process:

1 Create a new document.

2 **Save** this document.

3 **Close** down the application.

4 Open the existing document within the application at a later date.

There are two methods of opening an existing document.

1 Open the application and, from there, browse for the file.

2 Browse for the file. Double-click on the file. An application will be automatically opened according to its file extension; and the file is opened automatically within that application.

SAVE
See page 59.

CLOSE
See page 63.

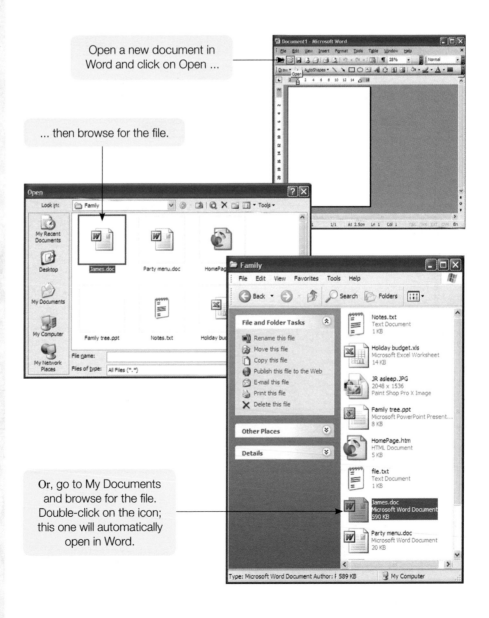

Open a new document in Word and click on Open ...

... then browse for the file.

Or, go to My Documents and browse for the file. Double-click on the icon; this one will automatically open in Word.

Open an existing document – from an application

If you have worked on the file recently, it might still be listed on the File drop-down menu.

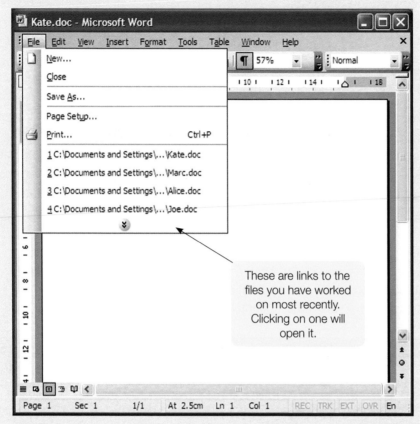

These are links to the files you have worked on most recently. Clicking on one will open it.

If not, there are three ways of opening an existing file from within an application:

 1 Select File/Open on the main menu toolbar.

 2 Click on the **Open icon**.

 3 Use the keyboard shortcut: Ctrl-O.

You then need to browse to locate the file, and double-click on it. Or, having selected the file, click on Open in the dialogue box.

YOUR TURN!

1 Open an application such as *Word*, and open an existing file that appears in your File drop-down menu.
2 Within the same application, click on the Open icon to open the Browse dialogue box. Then, browse to find a file to open. Notice that only files that can be opened within the application are listed.

OPEN ICON
See page 14.

DEMO
Your tutor will show you where to find files that have been created for you to work on in this course.

Opening files according to the file extension

FILE
EXTENSION
See page 35.

Sometimes, it is more convenient to locate documents first and then, according to the file type, and its **file extension**, to let the computer open the application for you.

HOW TO... **Open an existing document – and an application**

 1 Locate the file you want to open, by browsing through folders in My Documents.

 2 Right-click to open the context-sensitive menu.

 3 Click on Open.

For some files, you will be offered the option to Open With. This means you have more than one application which could be used. Pointing to Open With will reveal the options available to you.

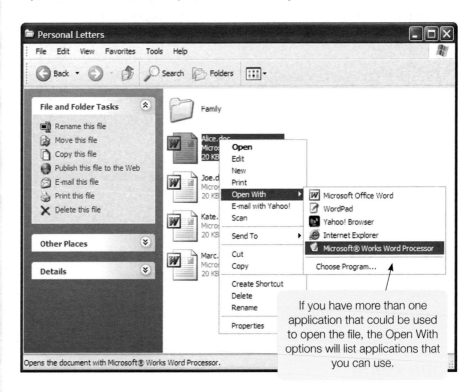

YOUR TURN!

1 Click on Start and open My Documents. Locate a file that you would like to open from My Documents. Select the file and use the Open option on the context-sensitive menu to open it.

Entering and editing text

When entering text – or editing text – you must position your cursor where you want to begin, and left-click.

Insert versus overtype

When you start to type, using a word processing package like *Word*, one of two things can happen.

 * The text is inserted – and any text to the right of the cursor moves to the right.
 * The text overtypes whatever was there already.

The Insert key is used to toggle between Insert and Overtype modes of input. To see which mode is in operation, look at the panel at the bottom of the *Word* workspace. You will see the following symbol OVR .

 * If OVR is greyed out, you are in Insert mode.
 * If OVR is black, you are in Overtype mode.

Inserting text

To insert text in *Word*, first make sure that OVR is not showing in the bottom panel; if it is, press the Insert key on the keyboard. Then type!

You don't need to – and should not – press the Enter key until you want to start a new paragraph. Wordwrap will move your text on to new lines for you automatically.

YOUR TURN!

1 Open *Word*, and create a new document. Using Insert mode, key in some text (approximately 200 words).
2 Position the cursor within your text and experiment with Overtype mode.
3 Use the Delete and Backspace keys to delete text.
4 Check that you know what effect other keys have:
Caps Lock, Shift and Tab.

! HANDY TIP
Depending on the software you are using, your cursor shape may change when you click.

REMEMBER
It was YOUR TURN! on page 27 to find out how to count the number of words.

Inserting images

Images are stored differently from text, but you can combine the two and have an image within a text document.

HOW TO... Insert an image

1 Select Insert/Picture on the main menu toolbar.

2 Choose the type of picture you plan to insert. In *Word*, this could be **Clip Art** or From File (i.e. an image that is stored in a file on your computer).

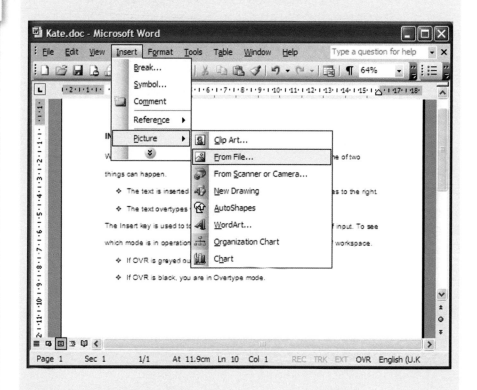

3 Browse to find the image that you want to include. Double-click on it, or select it and click Insert.

Formatting images

Once the image is within your document, you can format it.

Right-click on the image (or select Format/Picture) to open the Format Picture dialogue box.

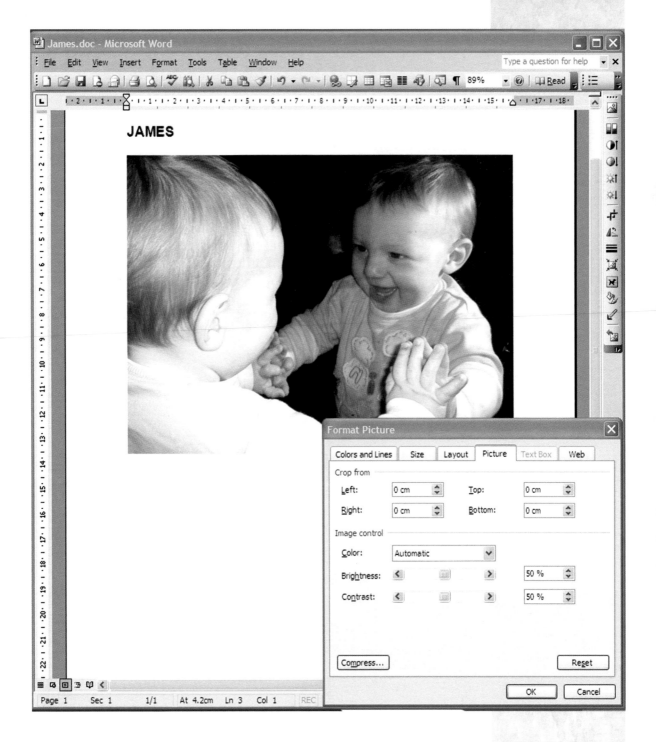

YOUR TURN!

1 Open an existing document and insert an appropriate picture or clip art into it.

2 Use the Format Picture option to change the size of the image.

3 Click on the image and use the mouse to drag the grab handles to change the size of the image, and to move the image on the page.

4 Experiment with using WordArt, a feature within *Word*, to create a letter heading, or the text for a poster.

DEMO

Your tutor will show you how you might use WordArt.

FONT

A particular shape of lettering of which there are two main types: san serif (without 'feet', e.g. Arial) or serif (with 'feet', e.g. Times Roman).

Formatting text – changing font size

The text can be styled so that it appears in a particular **font** and a particular size.

HOW TO... ## Change the font style and font size – method 1

 1 In a document, select the text that you want to change. (Click the mouse on the first character and drag it across the text, and then release the mouse button. This highlights the selected text.)

 2 Select Format/Font to open the dialogue box.

 3 Complete the entries, making all your choices, and click on OK.

You can choose a font ...

... and a font style like italic or bold ...

... and a point size.

You can also colour or underline your text ...

... and create special effects, like shadow.

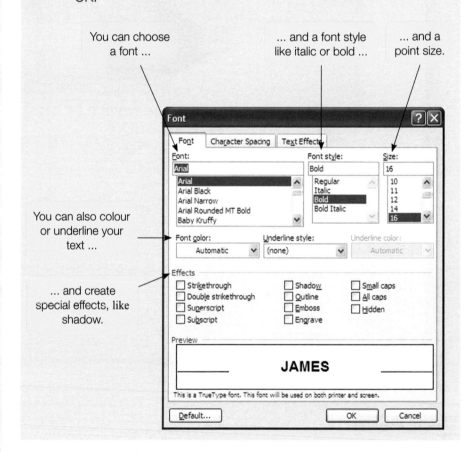

HOW TO... **Change the font style and font size
– method 2**

 1 Select (highlight) the text that you want to change.

2 On the Formatting toolbar, select the font style and font size
that you want to use.

Highlight the text you want to
format ...

... and then click on the arrow to reveal
options and select what you want.

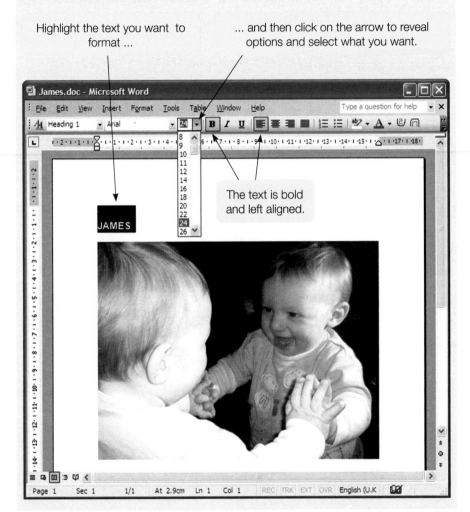

The text is bold
and left aligned.

 HOW TO... **Change the font style and font size
– method 3**

1 In *Word*, select (highlight) the text that you want to change.
Click on Format/Styles and Formatting to open the Styles and
Formatting panel.

 2 Select one of the predefined styles.

 3 You could modify the predefined style, or create a new style
altogether. Right-click on the style name to explore options.

⚠ WARNING! For
method 3, you
need a word
processing
package; a text
editor does not
offer styles.

LANDSCAPE
The longer side is along the top.
PORTRAIT
The shorter side is along the top.

Margins

When you create a new document, the application assumes default values for the size of paper and the amount of space to be left for margins.

If you want to change this, e.g. to print in **landscape** orientation instead of **portrait** orientation, or to use a different size of paper, you will need to amend the page setup.

 HOW TO... Change the page setup

 1 Select File/Page Setup to open the dialogue box.

2 Make your choices and click on OK.

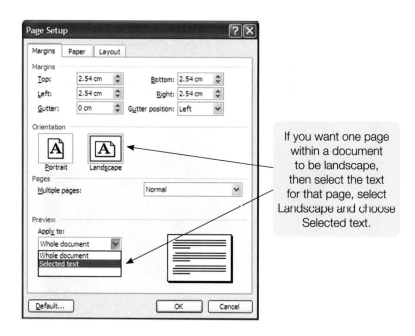

If you want one page within a document to be landscape, then select the text for that page, select Landscape and choose Selected text.

You can change the margins in Page Setup, but you can also change them in the workspace.

HOW TO... Change margins in the workspace

 1 If you cannot see a ruler along the top of your document and another down one side, select View/Rulers on the main menu toolbar.

 2 Position your cursor at the top or bottom of the side rule. This sets the top and bottom margins. When the cursor changes to a double-ended arrow, drag the margin to a new depth.

 3 Similarly, you can change the left and right margins by moving the markers on the top ruler.

Paragraph formatting

Individual characters of text can be formatted – font style, font size, bold, italic and underline, and so on.

Paragraphs can also be formatted. You can control the alignment of the text, and – if you are using a word processing package – the spacing between lines and before and after the paragraph, plus any indentation style.

Select Format/Paragraph to open the Paragraph dialogue box and to see all the options on offer to you.

Paragraph alignment

There are four options for alignment.

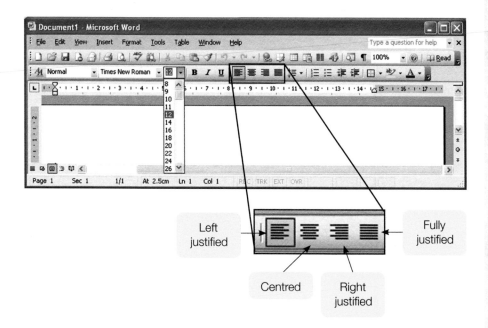

This text is **left justified**. The left-hand side of the text is aligned at the left-hand margin. The right-hand edge, though, is ragged.

This text is **right justified**. This is similar to left justified text, except that the left-hand side is ragged and the right-hand edge is aligned at the right-hand margin.

This text is **centred**.
An equal space is left at both ends of each line.
This is useful for posters and other notices.

Text may also be **fully justified**.   That means the text is stretched between the left and right margins, so there is no ragged right-hand margin.   This formatting is created by extra spaces being put between words.   It is important not to put two spaces after a full stop, otherwise justification can produce overlarge gaps in the text, as shown in this paragraph.

You can format the paragraph alignment using Format/Paragraph, but the icons for alignment of text are also all on the Formatting toolbar.

Highlight the text you want to align and click on the appropriate icon.

If you only want to style one paragraph, you can place the cursor anywhere within that paragraph – the highlighting step is not required.

YOUR TURN!

1 Using one of the methods explained on page 47, create a new document following the instructions below.

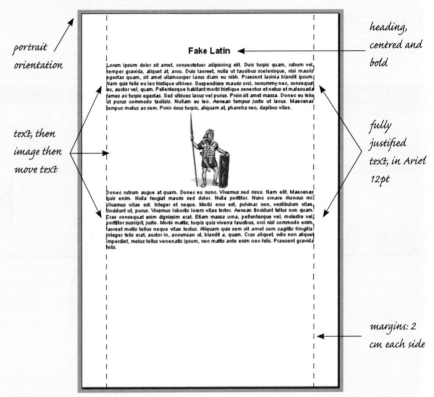

portrait orientation

text, then image then move text

heading, centred and bold

fully justified text, in Arial 12pt

margins: 2 cm each side

2 Use File/Page Setup to make sure the orientation is portrait; see page 56.

3 Using File/Page Setup or the rulers on the workspace (page 56), set the margins at 2cm on each side.

4 Make sure that you are in Insert mode and then type some paragraphs of text; see page 51.

5 Highlight all your text. This can be done using the shortcut Ctrl-A. Use Format/Font to format your text so that it appears in the Arial font, with **point size** 12. Set it fully justified.

6 Type a heading at the top of your text. Press Enter so that it appears on a line by itself. Move the cursor back up one line (using the mouse, or the arrow keys). Centre your heading, embolden it and use a large font size; see page 54.

7 Move your cursor to a point within the text where it would be appropriate to include an image. Insert an image and adjust its size so that it fits well, and balances the text; see page 52.

Saving files in different formats

When you have finished creating your document, or just need to stop because you have run out of time, you need to save your work.

It is also good practice to save your work regularly, rather than waiting until you have finished writing it.

Saving a file for the first time

When you create a new document, the application may offer a default name: *Word* calls any untitled document Document# where # is a number.

When you decide to save the file, *Word* offers you the first line of text as a default filename. This might be your heading, and may be a good name for the file. However, to give it a name that is more meaningful to you – so you can find it more easily later – select File/Save As … and complete the dialogue box.

! HANDY TIP
You can browse to place the file in a folder of your choice. You can even create a new folder into which to put it.

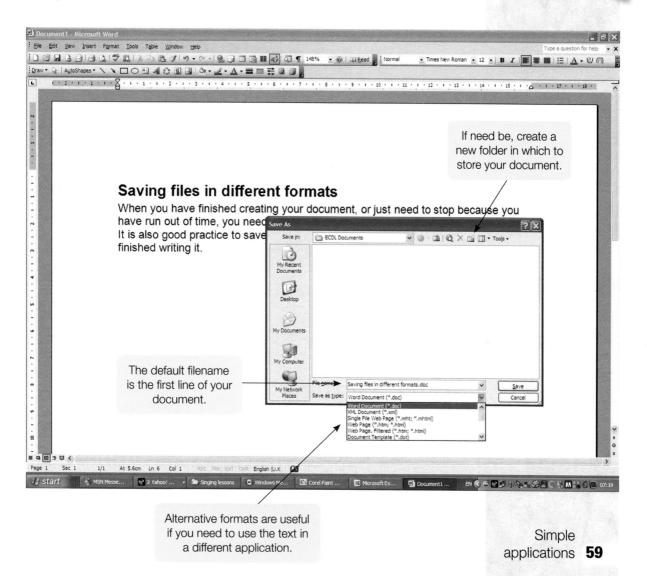

If need be, create a new folder in which to store your document.

The default filename is the first line of your document.

Alternative formats are useful if you need to use the text in a different application.

Saving a file – not for the first time

SAVE ICON
See page 14.

If your file already has a name that suits you, clicking on the **Save icon** (or selecting File/Save, or using the short cut key Ctrl-S) will overwrite the previous version on your disk.

The previous version will therefore not be available to you any more.

If you need to keep previous versions, for safety sake, or to keep a record of what changes were done, you need to use File/Save As and choose a new name for the file.

It will be saved in the default format for your application. For example, *Word* documents are saved with a **file extension** of .doc – these are called DOC files.

FILE EXTENSIONS
See page 35.

It makes sense to choose names that are similar, but to include a version number in the name, or the date and time it was created. If you save your file every so often, as a safety measure, at the end of the day you might have several files, and don't need to keep them all.

The next day you could delete all but the last version you created. The deleted files will be moved to your **Recycle Bin**, so if you should need them again you can restore them, anytime up to when you next empty the Recycle Bin.

RECYCLE BIN
See page 43.

YOUR TURN!

1 Create a new document and – using a meaningful name – save it in your ECDL folder as a Word document.

2 Open a document that already exists and save it under a different name in a new folder called Web documents, as a web document file. Save the file five more times, each time using a version number or the date and time you saved the file. Then, delete the earlier versions.

Printing

What does it mean?

HARD COPY
A printout on paper, rather than on the screen or on a disk.

If you have a printer connected to your computer, you can print a **hard copy** of your document.

Printer settings

To check that your work will be printed as you hoped, click on Start/Printers and Faxes to open the Printer dialogue box, and check the printer settings. The printer with the tick is the one where documents will be sent by default, and you need make sure it is ready for use.

❋ If it says 'Offline', check that your printer is turned on!

❋ If it says 'Ready', that's fine.

You can then close the Printer dialogue box.

Print Preview

To make sure your hard copy will look as planned, it makes sense to preview the document before you send it to the printer.

PRINT PREVIEW ICON
See page 14.

HOW TO... Preview a document

 1 Select File/Print Preview (or click on the Print Preview icon).

 2 This opens a viewing window, and you can look at each page separately. You can change margins and other settings.

DEMO
Your tutor will show you how to preview a document.

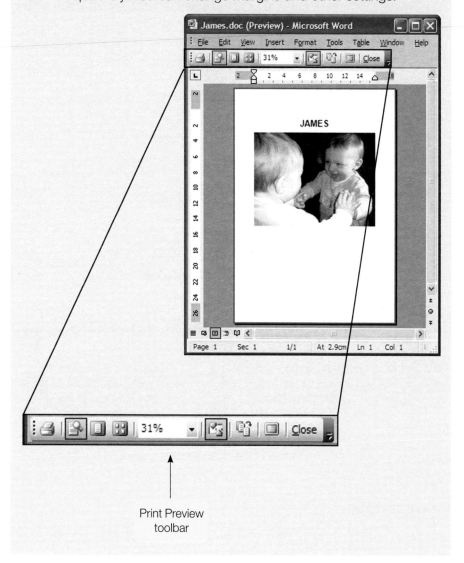

Print Preview toolbar

Printing a document

When you are happy that the document is ready to print, you can send it to the printer. First though, there are some options to decide and these settings can be changed by selecting File/Print and completing the dialogue box.

Which pages do you want to print?

How many copies of each page do you need?

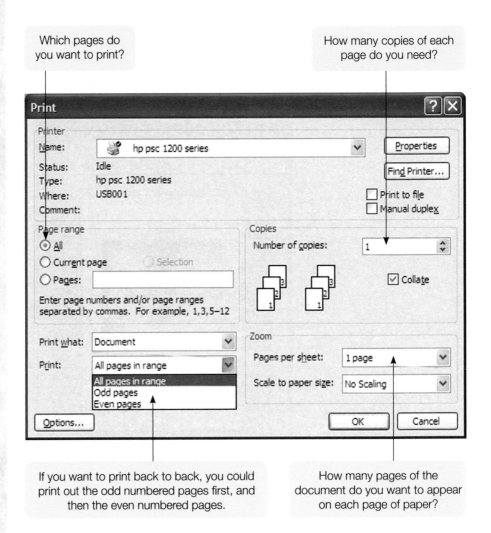

If you want to print back to back, you could print out the odd numbered pages first, and then the even numbered pages.

How many pages of the document do you want to appear on each page of paper?

If you want to print the whole document with the same settings as the last time you printed it, click on the **Print icon** on the Standard toolbar, or use the shortcut key Ctrl-P.

PRINT ICON
See page 14.

YOUR TURN!

1 Open a document and preview how it will look.

2 Open a document which has more than one page. Preview the document and print two copies of the last page only.

3 Create a new document. Type the word SILENCE. Change the orientation to landscape and increase the font size so that it fills the page. Preview the document and then, when you are happy, print one copy.

DEMO

Your tutor will show you how to create a document with more than one page, using page breaks.

Closing an application

Having too many applications open can slow down your computer. So, when you have finished working on an application, you should close it.

Pinning applications to the Start menu

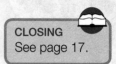
CLOSING
See page 17.

If you expect to use an application a lot, it will save you time if you pin it to the Start menu.

HOW TO... **Pin an application to the Start menu**

 1 Click on Start and locate the application.

 2 Right-click on the application name and select Pin to Start menu.

 3 To unpin an application, right-click and select Unpin.

The applications above the line are pinned to the Start menu.

The applications below the line are ones that you have used recently.

Right-click on the application that you want to pin to the Start menu, and choose Pin to Start menu.

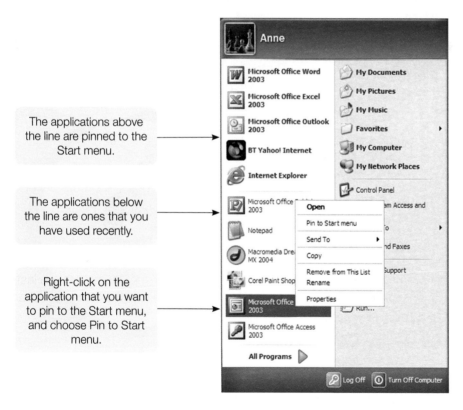

YOUR TURN!

1 Pin any applications that you plan to use regularly to your Start menu.

2 Close all applications.

3 Turn off your computer using the correct procedures.

Internet basics

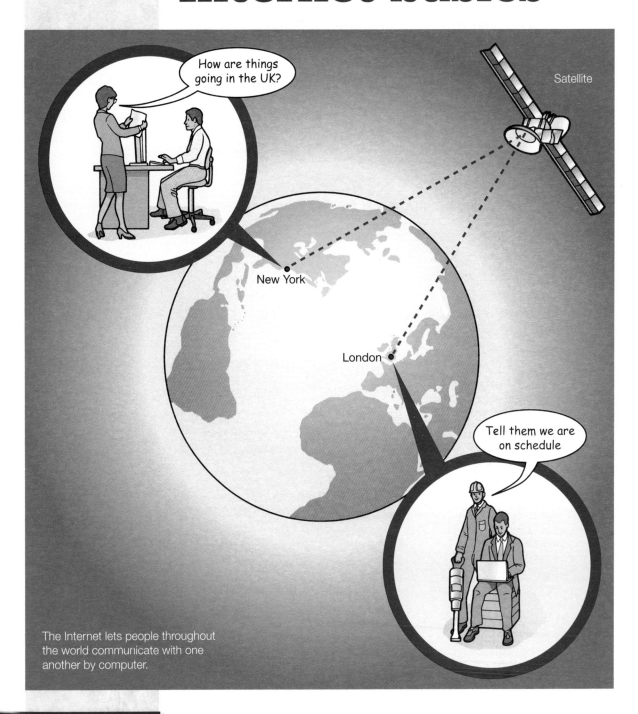

How are things going in the UK?

Satellite

New York

London

Tell them we are on schedule

The Internet lets people throughout the world communicate with one another by computer.

What is the Internet?

The Internet is a global network of millions of computers.

Each computer on the Internet is called a **node**.

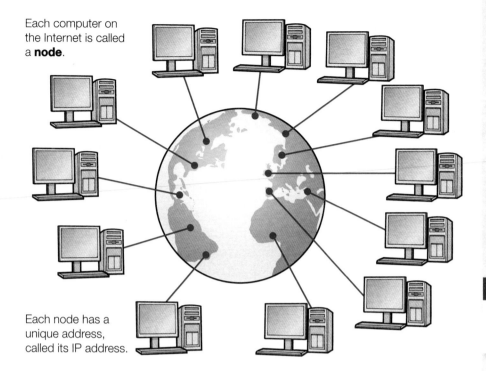

Each node has a unique address, called its IP address.

Internet hardware

Each computer on the Internet is linked so that anyone who is connected can access information, and communicate with other users on the Internet.

Internet uses

Now nearly 40 years old, the Internet allows communication between users and offers lots of services:

✳ E-mail, available since the early 1970s, is important enough to have its own section in this book (page 76).

✳ Newsgroups, chat rooms and bulletin boards provide 'meeting points' for like-minded people.

✳ The WWW is the way documents – web pages – are displayed on the Internet for all to see.

✳ Search engines, such as *Yahoo!* and *Google*, help researchers to access the wealth of information available on the WWW via the Internet.

✳ Nine areas of interest are considered in this book: news, government, consumer issues, travel, education and training, employment, health, interest groups and business.

What does it mean?

IP
Stands for Internet protocol.

! HANDY TIP
Block 2 of the e-Citizen syllabus is called 'Information Search', and pages 97–107 focus on how you would use the Internet to search for information.

E-Participation

The Internet can be used for everyday tasks like buying a CD or book, paying a bill, banking online or making a holiday reservation. You can also use the Internet to file your tax return, enrol on a course, make a doctor's appointment or take part in an online discussion forum.

Each of these activities involves electronic communication of information, some of it personal information. Often, it involves financially sensitive data.

Block 3 of the e-Citizen syllabus is called 'e-Participation' and pages 171–182 of this book focus on the options available, and the pitfalls that lie in wait for the unsuspecting Internet user.

DEMO

Your tutor will show you how to use the Drawing toolbar, how to set up tables, and how to use the spell checker.

YOUR TURN!

1 Open a new document in *Word* or another word processing package. Experiment with using the Drawing toolbar to draw a diagram to represent the Internet. Save your document in your ECDL folder, as 'Internet Diagram'. Print out one copy of your diagram, using portrait or landscape orientation as appropriate.

2 Open a new document. Experiment with inserting a table, with two columns and six rows. In the first row, use the columns headings: 'Uses' and 'Examples'. Use this table to display five uses of the Internet that interest you. Save your document as 'Internet Uses' in your ECDL folder.

What does it mean?

SPELL CHECKER
A software tool that compares words in a document with those in an electronically held dictionary.

3 Open a new document. Write a short description of things you would like to be able to do using the Internet. Use a **spell checker** to make sure there are no errors in your typing. Save your document as 'Internet plans' in your ECDL folder.

What is the WWW?

The World Wide Web (WWW) is a **hypermedia** system of web pages which has, embedded within it, hyperlinks that lead to other web pages. Because all these pages are ultimately linked, the WWW allows users to access the many millions of web pages that have been set up on the Internet.

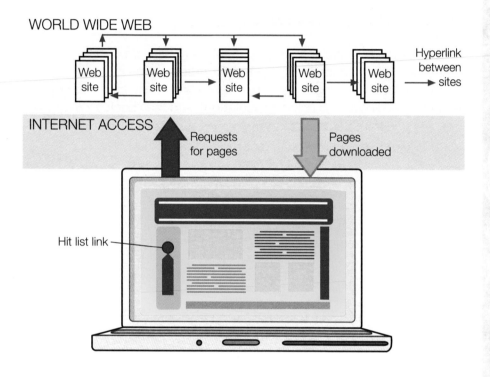

The web pages are written in a special language called **HTML** and users need a **browser** to access these websites and interpret the HTML. The *Microsoft* browser is called *Internet Explorer*.

YOUR TURN!

1 Open the file called 'Internet Diagram' (it should be in your ECDL folder) and amend the diagram to include the WWW. Save the file as 'Internet and WWW diagram'.

2 Insert a heading, and write a paragraph explaining the difference between the Internet and the WWW.

3 Save your document with a name that indicates the version. Print out a copy of your document.

BROWSER
See page 72.

REMEMBER to Print Preview your work before printing.

What does it mean?

BROADBAND
A fast connection between computers along telephone lines.

ISP
Stands for Internet service provider.

The hardware and software

To link your computer to the Internet, you need some special hardware and software (see below, and next page).

You also need a way to connect your computer to the Internet, e.g. through a telephone line, cable, or satellite. You may have **Broadband** and/or a wireless connection.

Finally, you also need to subscribe to an **ISP** such as *AOL* or *BT Yahoo!*.

Internet hardware

What does it mean?

MODEM
A hardware device that modulates and demodulates a computer signal.

To send data files – such as e-mails or web pages – from one computer to another via a telephone line, you need a **modem**. The modem converts the signals that the computer creates into ones that can be sent along the telephone line (this is called **modulation**), and then back again at the receiving end (called **demodulation**).

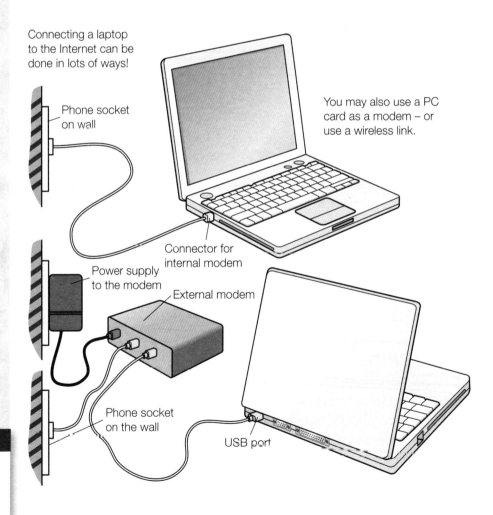

Connecting a laptop to the Internet can be done in lots of ways!

Phone socket on wall

You may also use a PC card as a modem – or use a wireless link.

Connector for internal modem

Power supply to the modem

External modem

Phone socket on the wall

USB port

What does it mean?

USB (UNIVERSAL SERIAL BUS)
A fast connector for peripherals, such as modems, mice and external storage devices.

The modem may be internal (housed within your computer processor box) or external. An external modem may be connected to a **USB** port; it may also be used for broadband connection.

Internet software

The communications software used to access web pages is called a **browser**: a package that displays pages that have been created in Web format. The browser is needed to read the HTML code in which web pages are written.

The two most common browsers are *Microsoft Internet Explorer* and *Netscape*.

BROWSER
See page 72.

BT Yahoo! personalises the home page for its subscribers. You can choose what appears on the page ...

... news ...

... horoscopes ...

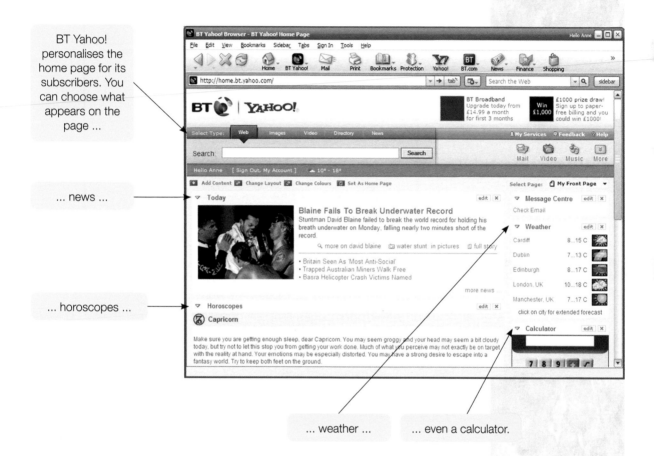

... weather ...

... even a calculator.

YOUR TURN!

1 Discuss with others in your group what hardware and software you have at home, or at your place of work. How is your computer connected to the Internet? Make notes and sketch diagrams.

2 Open a new document in *Word* or some other word processing package. List the equipment that you need to connect to the Internet. Save your document as 'Internet hardware' in your ECDL folder.

3 Open a new document in *Word* or some other word processing package. Write a short description of the role of an ISP. Format your text and print out one copy. Save the file as 'ISP' in your ECDL folder.

REMEMBER
to Print Preview your work before you print it out.

Web addresses

SEARCH
ENGINE
See page 98.

To use the WWW efficiently and effectively, you need to be able to locate websites of interest as quickly as possible.

To discover new and relevant sites, you need to search the WWW, using a **search engine** such as *Google*.

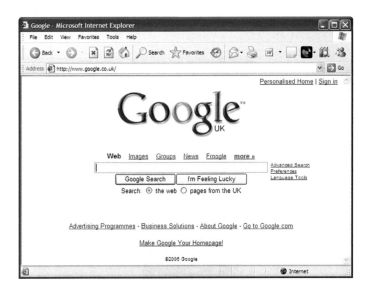

What does it mean?

URL
Stands for universal resource locator.

For sites that you have visited before, you need to retain the **URLs** – or web address – so that you can visit them again.

* You can **bookmark** pages that are of particular interest to you. These URLs are stored in your Favorites folder.

* Or you can refer to your **History folder**, which keeps a list of all the URLs of all websites that you have visited recently.

BOOKMARK
See page 115.

Click on the History icon to reveal the History panel.

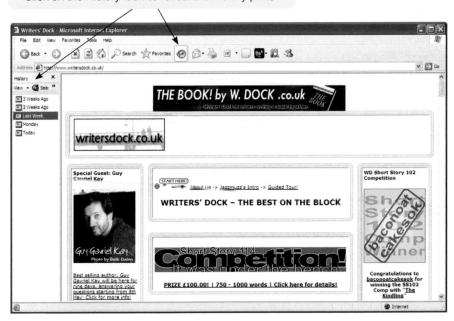

URLs

To access a website on the WWW you need its URL, for example http://www.bbc.co.uk/health/.

The URL usually starts with **http://**. This is the **protocol** that will be used by the browser to interpret the HTML code and display the web page on your screen.

The next bit (the **domain name**: www.bbc.co.uk) tells you something about whose website you will be viewing. The last bit of the domain name tells you the type of organisation (government, company, organisation) – and the country of origin (UK, France …) – of the website owner.

Finally, the URL specifies a page or image within the site (e.g. /health/). If nothing appears after the domain name, the URL defaults to the home page of the website.

What does it mean?

HTTP
Stands for hypertext transfer protocol.

PROTOCOL
An agreed set of rules.

Organisation	Website addresses
News	www.news.independent.co.uk www.indymedia.org
Government	www.direct.gov.uk www.businesslink.gov.uk
Consumer issues	www.ofcom.org.uk
Travel	www.expedia.co.uk www.thetrainline.com
Education and training	www.heinemann.co.uk www.dfes.gov.uk
Employment	www.jobcentreplus.gov.uk
Health	www.bbc.co.uk/health/ www.bupa.co.uk
Interest groups	www.writersdock.co.uk
Business	www.business.timesonline.co.uk

YOUR TURN!

1 Find more examples of websites in the nine areas that you will focus on during this course. Look in newspapers, on headed notepaper, in advertising on TV and in magazines. Make a note of their URLs.

2 Study the way the URLs are composed. Look for variety in the tail end of the URL.

What does it mean?

BROWSER
Software that gets
pages from the WWW
and displays them on
your screen.

Using URLs to access web pages

When you sign up with an ISP, you will be provided with a **browser** – such as *Microsoft Internet Explorer* or *Netscape* – to access the WWW via the Internet.

The workspace of the browser includes features that will help you to access particular websites.

Main menu

Standard browser buttons

Address bar

Favorites panel of bookmarked websites

Scroll bars are needed to view the full width and depth of some web pages.

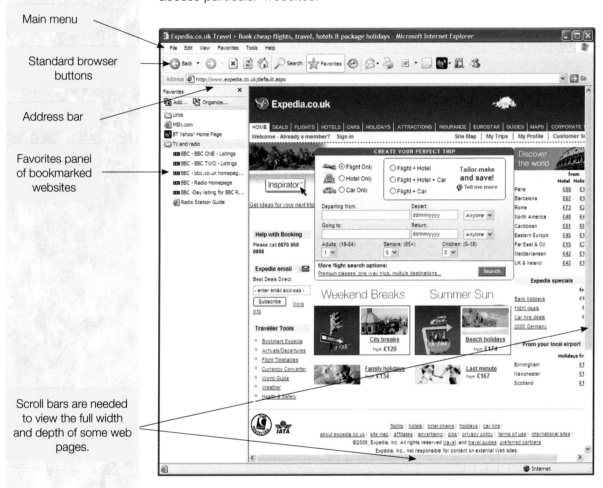

Standard browser buttons

You will learn to use the standard browser buttons like Back and Forward later (page 75).

You will also learn on page 115 how to add website URLs to your favourites by bookmarking them.

Address bar

The address bar is where you need to enter the URL.

As you start to key in the characters, you are presented with a drop-down list of sites that have similar names.

Selecting one of these (by clicking on it) can save you time, and cut down the chances of you making a mistake.

When you have finished entering the URL, press Enter, or click on Go, to go to this page.

Home page

The home page of the browser is the first page you see when you open the browser application. You can set this to be any page you like. So, if you want to start your Internet day by looking at the news, you could choose the website of a newspaper, or of the BBC.

REMEMBER
If the URL ends with the domain name, it will default to the home page of the website.

HOW TO... **Select your own home page for your browser**

 1 Open the browser.

 2 Go to the site you want to use for your home page by entering the URL in the address bar and pressing Enter.

3 Wait until the page has fully downloaded.

 4 Select Tools/Internet Options.
Select 'Use Current' and click OK.

! HANDY TIP
A web page downloads in stages, and progress is shown in the bottom left of your screen. It says 'Done' when the download is complete.

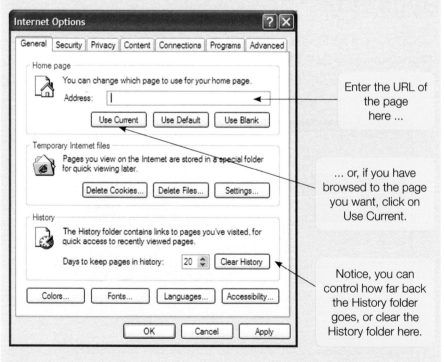

Enter the URL of the page here ...

... or, if you have browsed to the page you want, click on Use Current.

Notice, you can control how far back the History folder goes, or clear the History folder here.

 5 There is an option to select the current page as your home page. Or you can enter the URL of the site you want to see each time you open your browser.

YOUR TURN!

1 Open your Internet browser application.

2 Study the toolbars and roll the cursor over each icon to identify each one. Notice, in particular, the icons for Back, Forward, Favorite and History.

3 In the address bar, enter the URL for one of the sites listed in the table on page 71, and go to that site.

4 In the address bar, enter another URL and press Go.

5 Click on the History icon to view the sites you have visited recently.

6 Select a site to use for your home page, and set this up. Close the application and reopen it to check that your home page is as hoped.

Navigating the Web

When you visit a website, the site may have lots of pages, each one providing different information for you to view. Moving from page to page is called navigating the website. There are a number of ways to do this.

❋ **Browser buttons** can take you back and forth through pages you have viewed already.

❋ **Hyperlinks** can be used to jump to new places within a website or to another website altogether.

Hyperlinks

DEMO

Your tutor will show you how to use textual hyperlinks to navigate a website.

Web designers can include text and images which, when clicked, take you to another place in the same website, or to a new website altogether.

So that you can spot these hyperlinks, such textual links are usually displayed in a different colour and/or in a different font, and they are often underlined.

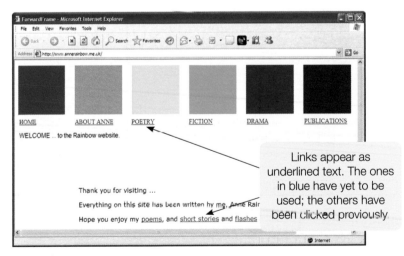

Links appear as underlined text. The ones in blue have yet to be used; the others have been clicked previously.

When you roll the cursor over an image or icon that is used as a hyperlink, the image or icon usually changes in some way so you can tell it is a link. A message might even appear telling you where the hyperlink will take you. And the pointer shape may also change, e.g. to a pointing finger.

Browser buttons

Browser buttons appear at the top of your workspace on the Standard toolbar.

Each page that you view is downloaded into a temporary folder and this takes time. If you want to flick back and forwards between web pages that have already been downloaded, you can, very quickly, using the **Back** ⊙ and **Forward** ⊙ buttons.

Because you are then viewing versions of the pages that were downloaded earlier, the pages might not be as up to date as they could be. To see an up-to-date version of a particular page, navigate to it (using Back or Forward) and click the **Refresh** button ⟳ . You will then have to wait for that page to be downloaded again. If a page is taking ages to download, the **Stop** button ⊗ can be used to cancel the request for that page.

Clicking the **Home** icon ⌂ takes you to the page you have chosen as your **Home page**.

Clicking on a **Search** icon ⌕ Search opens a new window or panel, depending on the software application, so you can find information of interest to you on the WWW.

The **Favorites** icon ☆ Favorites reveals the Favorites panel (or bookmark folder depending on your software application) which retains the URLs of sites you decide you want to visit again.

The browser software keeps track of all pages that you visit and puts the URLs for these sites in your History folder. Clicking on the **History** icon ⊙ reveals the list of links for the recent past.

The **Mail** icon ⊠▾ takes you to your inbox so that you can check your e-mails. For example, in *Internet Explorer* it can take you to your inbox in *Outlook*. In *BTYahoo!*, it reveals your inbox within that software.

Clicking on the **Print** icon ⎙ sends the web page you are looking at to the printer.

The **Edit with Microsoft Word** icon ▧ ▾ puts the content of the current web page into *Word*. You can then use the text in some way, editing it to suit your needs.

YOUR TURN!

1 Open your browser application. Use the History folder to go to a website that you have visited before. Explore the chosen website, using hyperlinks to visit at least three other pages within the site.

2 Use the Back and Forward buttons to revisit all the pages that you have viewed so far.

3 For one page, click on the Refresh button to download an up-to-date version of the page. While this is being downloaded, notice the messages displayed in the bottom left-hand corner of your browser window.

4 Look for a page that offers links to other websites and follow such a hyperlink. Notice what address is shown in the address bar.

5 Click on the Home button and then close the browser application.

DEMO

Your tutor will show you how the pointer shape may change when you roll the cursor over a hyperlink.

DEMO

Your tutor will show you how to use the browser buttons to navigate a website.

What does it mean?

HOME PAGE
See page 73.
SEARCHING
See page 97.
BOOKMARKING
See page 115.
HISTORY FOLDER
See page 000.

What does it mean?

PRINTING A WEB PAGE
See page 113.
COPYING A WEB PAGE
See page 111.

E-mail basics

In this section, you will learn how to use your computer to communicate using e-mails.

What is e-mail?

E-mail is an electronic communication system available for sending a message from one user to another through the Internet.

Both the sender and the recipient need to have access to the Internet. Unlike telephone communication, though, they do not have to be online at the same time.

Each user needs to have an e-mail address (page 78) and to know the addresses of people they want to send e-mails to. The addresses can be stored in an **e-mail address book**.

At the present time, users may pay to subscribe to an ISP which includes the provision of e-mail addresses, and then users are free to send as many e-mails as they like, at no extra cost. However, recent debate among ISPs suggests that, now that everyone is used to sending lots of e-mails, a small charge per e-mail – similar to that being charged to send a text message by mobile phone – might be levied.

E-mail versus snail mail – the mechanics

Sending mail through the postal system – by **snail mail** – is a slow process compared with the e-mail alternative.

With snail mail, you need to write your letter on paper, put it in an envelope, address the envelope and put a stamp on it. You post the letter one day and, overnight, the postal service moves the mail to a sorting office near the addressee. Eventually – hopefully the next day – the letter is delivered through the letter box of the addressee.

If, instead, you use e-mail, all the details (the address of the person you are sending it to, the subject and your message) are completed on your computer screen. When you click on Send, the message is delivered almost instantly to the inbox of the intended recipient. That person can access the message next time he or she logs on.

What does it mean?

E-MAIL
Short for 'electronic mail'.

E-MAIL ADDRESS BOOK
See page 91.

REMEMBER
ISP stands for Internet service provider.

What does it mean?

SNAIL MAIL
An affectionate term for the postal delivery system used for 'normal' mail.

YOUR TURN!

1 This table compares e-mail with snail mail. Working as a group, consider other pros and cons of e-mail and snail mail.

E-mail versus snail mail	
Paper	There is no need for you to print out your e-mail, nor for the person receiving it to do so; this saves time, paper and printing costs.
Attachments	With an e-mail, files of any format can be attached, e.g. you can attach a simple document or a jpeg graphic. If you wanted to do the same with a letter going through the post, you would have to save the file on to a CD and pay the extra postage costs involved because of the increased weight. Your CD may or may not be returned, so this may incur extra costs too.
Location	With 'normal' mail, you have to know the location of the addressee – a post code which indicates their home or office. If the person is away on holiday, or ill in hospital, you are not to know, and the envelope may lie on their doormat, unopened, until they return. With e-mail, a person can pick up their messages from any location in the world – provided they have Internet access.
Timing	E-mails can be sent at any hour, not according to collection times. E-mails can also be collected at any time, not just when the post is delivered to your home or office.

DEMO

Your tutor will show you how to turn text into a list style of formatting.

2 Create a new document using a word processing application. List your own ideas. Save the file in your ECDL folder.

E-mail addresses

! HANDY TIP

If you know the e-mail address of one employee, you should be able to guess the e-mail addresses of others working for the same organisation.

An **e-mail address** is a string of characters, such as **johnsmith235@btinternet.com**, that uniquely identifies a user. Companies that arrange for all their staff to have e-mail addresses adopt a set pattern for the part before the @ symbol. This may be **<firstname>_<surname>** or **<initial><dot><surname>** or some other pattern.

Notice that the tail end of an e-mail address is similar to the tail end of a website address. If you amend the front end – up to and including the @ symbol – to 'http://www.' you will probably have the web address of the organisation responsible for issuing the e-mail address.

If you set up a personal e-mail account, such as a Hotmail account, and choose an e-mail address that has already been allocated, you will be offered an alternative; maybe a similar one with a number tacked on. The @ symbol within an e-mail address separates the 'name' of the person from the **domain name** of an organisation that looks after those people's e-mails.

DOMAIN NAME
See page 71.

YOUR TURN!

1 Visit some of the websites that you have visited before. Navigate to a page within each site that offers contact details. Note the e-mail addresses that are offered, and compare these with the URL of the site.

2 Within your group, swap work e-mail addresses. Notice how they are composed. What does the e-mail address tell you about each company or organisation?

3 Guess the website addresses for the employers of others in your group. Visit these sites and look at the contact page. Notice if there is a particular pattern in how e-mail addresses for employees are created.

REMEMBER
Your History folder shows the URLs of the sites you have visited before. Left-click a link to go to any particular website.

Terminology

E-mail seems to involve a lot of terminology. How many of these questions make sense to you?

✳ What is the role of an ISP?

✳ How can you set up and use an e-mail account?

✳ What is **junk mail**? How can you stop junk mail arriving in your inbox?

✳ What is a **virus**? What impact might a virus have on your computer? How can viruses spread? What can you do to prevent this?

These questions are answered in the next few pages.

REMEMBER
ISP stands for Internet service provider

What does it mean?

JUNK MAIL
This is unsolicited mail – usually you do not want to receive this mail.

What is the role of an ISP?

To gain access to the Internet, you need to subscribe to an ISP, and install their software on your computer.

Some ISPs offer a 'free' service; others charge a monthly subscription fee.

ISP software is often preloaded on to newly purchased computers, and you simply have to connect through your modem to register use of the service. For some ISPs, you may have to download additional software to access the full range of features on offer.

VIRUSES
See page 81.

Setting up an e-mail account

Having chosen your ISP, and arranged a subscription or free service, you need to choose a unique e-mail address, and set up your e-mail account on your computer.

Setting up the account involves following instructions given by your ISP, so that your computer has the necessary settings for e-mails addressed to you to arrive in your inbox, and for those you have composed to be taken from your outbox and delivered to the inboxes of your addressees.

DEMO

Your tutor will show you how to set up a web-based e-mail account.

Junk mail

Junk mail (or **spam**) is unsolicited mail, sent by someone you don't know already, and that you usually do not want to receive. Sending such mail through the postal service can be expensive; electronically, it is very cheap. It is usually done to advertise something, but sometimes is nothing more than mischief making. It takes up bandwidth on the Internet, may clog up systems, and takes time to remove.

What does it mean?

SPAM
This is another name for junk mail.

Most ISPs now provide a **spam filter** to trap potential junk e-mails. These e-mails are put into a separate e-mail inbox, called 'Bulk' or 'Junk'. You can 'train' the filter by identifying e-mails that are not spam. However, the first time you receive an e-mail that has been sent to lots of people, e.g. from a club you belong to, it will probably land in the Bulk/Junk e-mail inbox. So check this folder at least once a week – just in case.

DEMO

Your tutor will show you how to check your Bulk e-mail inbox, and how to train your spam filter.

There are 4 unopened e-mails in the Bulk inbox.

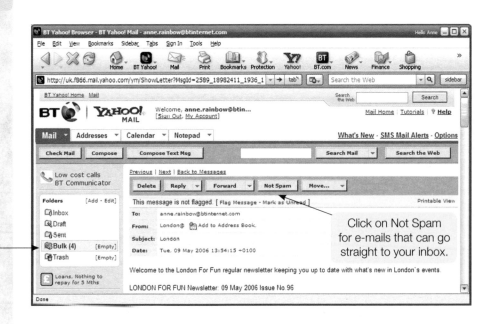

Click on Not Spam for e-mails that can go straight to your inbox.

YOUR TURN!

1 Find out what options you have to prevent spam reaching your e-mail inbox.

2 Look in your Bulk e-mail inbox. Identify any mail that is not spam, so that it can be transferred to your non-spam inbox.

Viruses and similar threats

Viruses can cause damage to computers. These programs are designed to delete or alter other programs on your computer, or to corrupt data in some way.

Most people who suffer a virus attack experience loss of both data and access to their computer for as long as it takes to fix. A virus infection represents an inconvenience to most individuals, but can have devastating effects on an organisation which relies on its computer system for business transactions.

A virus is a piece of software code – a program – that, when run, causes unexpected things to happen; these are usually negative events such as the deletion of part of your hard disk. A virus can also replicate itself, and thus spread.

* **Computer worms** are also viruses; they live in the active memory of your computer. They may send copies of themselves through e-mail or **IRC**, and so can spread very quickly from one computer to another.

* A **Trojan horse** program is similar to a virus in that it is written to cause damage to your computer, but it cannot replicate itself, so it is not classed as a virus. However, it can be equally destructive, so this distinction between viruses and Trojans is often overlooked.

Viruses, like hurricanes, are given names. The anti-virus software vendors have constructed huge databases containing information on all known viruses with advice as to the level of risk expected and how to recover from an attack.

One famous virus – the Melissa virus – spread very quickly, overwhelming commercial, government and military computer systems.

What does it mean?

IRC
Stands for Internet relay chat.

How viruses infect a PC

Viruses/Trojan horses/worms (see the table on page 120) can be introduced to a PC by any of three sources:

* If you save data on to a floppy disk from one PC that is infected with a virus, then, when you read that floppy into a second PC, the virus can infect the second PC. This can happen when a file is opened from the floppy, or when you boot from the floppy disk.

* Files can arrive at a PC as attachments to e-mails. If the file was saved from a PC that was infected, the receiving PC can become infected as soon as the attached file is opened.

* Viruses may also be hidden within files that you download from the WWW. While your ports are open for a legitimate transfer, other material may arrive and infect your computer.

Because viruses are programs, they can only infect programs. However, having done so, they can wipe files from your hard disk and/or make your PC crash, and can even make it become inoperable.

Virus protection is essential if you plan to connect to the Internet. This can take the form of anti-virus software and/or a firewall.

VIRUS
PROTECTION
See page 82.

REMEMBER

You can opt to show or hide file extensions as a Folder Option.

Viruses – double file extensions

Some viruses hide by using a double file extension.

In a file called harmlessfun.jpg.vbs, the 'vbs' part shows that it is a Visual Basic program – and a potential virus.

But, if you have opted to hide file extensions, it will show in a folder listing as harmlessfun.jpg and look just like an image file to you.

Virus protection software

Almost at the same rate as virus writers invent new viruses, so do anti-virus software vendors produce updated versions of their software.

Virus protection software attempts to trace viruses by looking for the **virus signature**. Meanwhile, virus writers adopt **cloaking** techniques.

The only defence against viruses is to subscribe to a reliable anti-virus software vendor's virus protection service.

Regular scanning of the PC is recommended, as is immediate update of virus software as soon as it is released.

What does it mean?

VIRUS PROTECTION SOFTWARE
Attempts to trap viruses and therefore prevent them from damaging data and software.

VIRUS SIGNATURE
A feature of a virus that identifies it.

CLOAKING
Hiding behind some disguise.

Virus protection: DAT files

The anti-virus software vendors maintain a database of information about viruses: a DAT file of their profiles and signatures. Users who subscribe to an online anti-virus protection service may have this database downloaded to their PC automatically each time an update is released. Other users may receive an e-mail telling them that an update is available.

Having the most up-to-date DAT file, scanning regularly and avoiding opening e-mails that might contain viruses is all that PC users can do to protect themselves. You need to perform anti-virus checks as part of a regular maintenance programme. And, if your system behaves strangely, you may have a virus, so do a scan!

What does it mean?

RESCUE DISK
This emergency disk contains enough software to restart your PC, plus anti-virus software so that you can clean an infected PC.

Virus protection: rescue disk

Anti-virus software vendors may include the option to create a **rescue disk**. If your system fails due to a virus and will not boot, this rescue disk should solve the problem.

Write-protecting a disk will prevent it becoming infected with a virus.

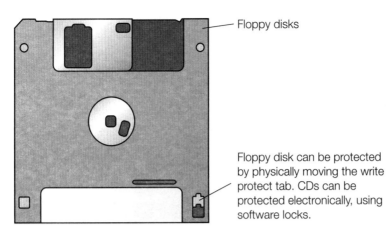

Floppy disks

Floppy disk can be protected by physically moving the write protect tab. CDs can be protected electronically, using software locks.

YOUR TURN!

1 Visit the site www.dti.gov.uk/publications/ and browse by subject for publications about information security management. Make notes.

2 Share experiences of virus attack with others in your group. What damage was done? How did you recover from the attack? What lessons did you learn?

3 Create a rescue disk. Write-protect the disk.

HOW TO... Perform a virus check

 1 Your anti-virus protection needs to be as up to date as possible. Go online to your anti-virus software provider and use their facilities to check to see whether an update is necessary. (Some vendors offer to advise you automatically, and to download updates automatically, whenever you are online. You should accept such offers; it saves you having to remember to check for updates, and reduces the amount of time that your PC may be unprotected from the latest viruses.)

 2 Once you are sure that you have the best anti-virus data available to you, use the anti-virus software menu to select the virus scan option.

3 You will be asked to identify which parts of your ICT-based system you want to be checked. You might want to check for viruses only on a floppy disk, or a CD, from which you intend to read files. You should, however, on a regular basis, check your hard disk for viruses too. Mark the relevant boxes to show which drives are to be checked for viruses, and then click OK.

 4 If a virus is found during the scan, your anti-virus software will attempt to clean the file for you. Sometimes, it is not possible to clean the file and it may have to be deleted. If it is an important systems file, you may need to reinstate it – from your backup files.

YOUR TURN!

1 Use anti-virus software to perform a scan of your hard disk.

2 Make a backup of important files.

DEMO
Your tutor will show you how to set up a rescue disk.

DEMO
Your tutor will show you how to do a virus check.

REMEMBER
Your anti-virus protection includes software as well as the DAT files which contain information on known viruses.

What does it mean?

BACKUP
For safety sake, it makes sense to keep a copy of all important files; these are called backup files.

DEMO
Your tutor will show you how to back up your files.

Creating an e-mail message

What does it mean?

WEBMAIL
E-mail services available via the WWW, such as a Hotmail account.

To use e-mail facilities, you can use **webmail** or you may decide to install an e-mail client software package, such as *Microsoft Outlook*. This may offer more control over who might access your confidential correspondence. There are other considerations though. Here are some pros and cons of using webmail services as opposed to e-mail client services.

Webmail	Client service such as Outlook
Your address book and copies of incoming and outgoing mail are stored on the server, not on your computer.	Your address book and copies of incoming and outgoing mail are stored on your computer. This takes up space.
You only have access to them when you are connected to the Internet, which may be costly.	You can process e-mails offline. This may save you money.
You can use the Internet anywhere in the world, and access your e-mails from any PC.	If you try to work online but without using your own PC (e.g. from an Internet café) you would not have access to all your addresses.

If your computer has a browser loaded, you may already have an e-mail package installed: for example, *Microsoft Internet Explorer* uses an e-mail client called *Outlook Express*.

There are other e-mail clients available, and they will usually work with the most common browser software.

All e-mail services – whichever one you choose to use – will offer the standard functions: creating, replying to and forwarding e-mails.

What does it mean?

FORM
A screen full of data fields laid out for easy completion so as to collect data from the user.

Creating an e-mail from scratch involves completing a **form** onscreen.

✳ Some of the fields – like the To field – are compulsory, so you have to complete them before sending your e-mail.

✳ Some are optional – like the fields for CC and BCC; you may leave them blank.

✳ You can complete the fields in any order you like.

When you have created your e-mail, depending on how your e-mail application is set up, the message goes first to your outbox, and will then be sent from your computer when you are next sending/receiving mail. Or it might go straight away – or as soon as you are online again.

1 Open your e-mail application. You may also have to log on and enter a password.

 2 Start the creation process. This may mean clicking on a Compose button, or selecting New/Mail message on a menu.

 3 Complete the fields on the form.

 4 **Attach a file** if you like.

 5 Read through what you have written to check you are happy with the wording, and your spelling.

 6 Then, press Send!

ATTACHING FILES
See page 89.

Click on Compose to start a new e-mail.

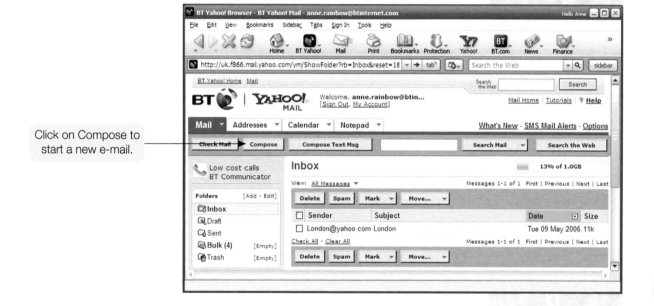

Include a subject line here . . .

. . . and write your message here.

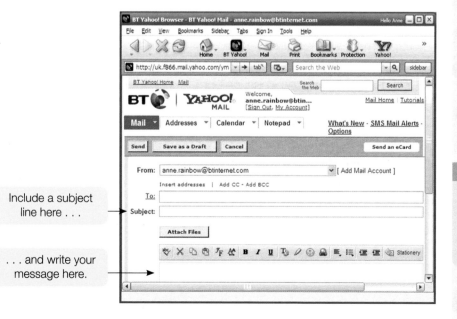

DEMO

Your tutor will show you how to complete all the fields for your e-mail, and how to use your address book.

ADDRESS BOOK
See page 91.

The To field

You can type the e-mail address of the person your e-mail is to go to. However, you might make a mistake. It is safer to use information from your **address book**.

You can address your new e-mail to more than one person, and if there is a group of people to whom you send the same e-mails you should consider setting up a **distribution list**.

The CC field

If you want someone else to receive a copy of your e-mail – for information only – include their name in the CC field. The recipient (in the To field) will see who has been copied in, and so will be aware that the e-mail is not private.

The BCC field

If you want to copy someone in but don't want the other recipient(s) to know, use the BCC field.

The Subject field

It helps to include a meaningful subject line for each e-mail. If the recipient replies, it is most likely that the subject line will read 'Re: …' and repeat your subject field entry, making it easier to locate messages that belong to one 'conversation'.

YOUR TURN!

1 Check that you know how to open your e-mail application. If you are using webmail, you will need to go online and have your logon/password details ready.

2 Locate the Compose button, or the way of creating a new e-mail. Experiment with completing the fields for a new e-mail. Which ones are compulsory?

3 Send an e-mail to someone in your group. Did they receive it?

4 Investigate, using online help, how to set up a distribution list using your e-mail software. Make sure you can add new addresses to the group, and delete them.

5 Experiment with sending an e-mail to a group of friends using a distribution list that you have set up.

Opening an e-mail

When e-mails are sent to you, they arrive in your **inbox**.

You may be able to tell which ones have been read and which have not; the unread ones may be in bold, and there may be an icon of an envelope that is closed for unread e-mails and open for ones you have read.

If you want to read what the e-mail says, you will need to select the e-mail. Web-based e-mails can then be opened with a single-click.

What does it mean?

INBOX
On arrival, e-mails are put in an inbox – a special folder set up by the e-mail software.

You can hide/show the preview panel by clicking on this button.

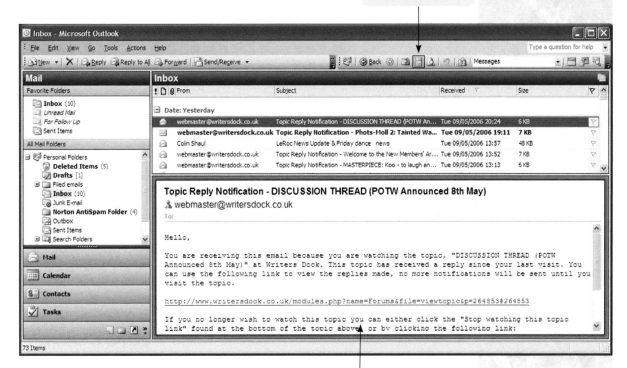

Some e-mail software offers a preview panel. This allows you to read a message without opening it by single clicking on it. Double clicking will open the e-mail in a new window.

REMEMBER
You do not have to open an e-mail. It may be safer to delete the e-mail without looking at its contents.

YOUR TURN!

1 Check your inbox to see if there is any mail for you. Notice the icons which indicate whether an e-mail has been opened.

2 Find out if your software offers a preview panel.

3 Delete any e-mails that you have read and want to discard, and any that you have decided not to read at all.

Sending an e-mail

Having created a new e-mail, and completed all the necessary fields on the e-mail form, you send it, by clicking on the Send button.

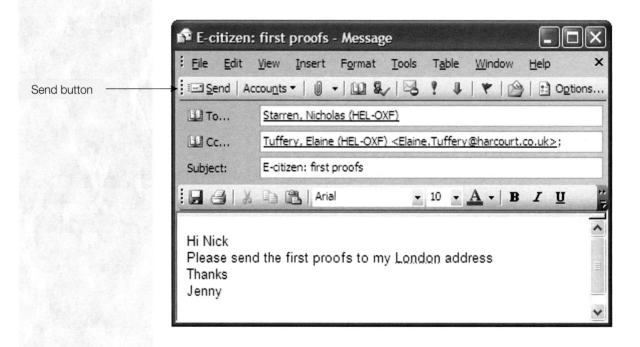

Send button

Pressing Send puts the e-mail message in your **outbox**. With some setups, your e-mail message will be despatched straight away. However, you may be able to set up your system so that the mail is despatched later, next time you are online.

If you are paying for online access by the minute, it makes sense to create and process e-mails offline, and only go online for long enough to send e-mails from your outbox and accept the next incoming batch into your inbox.

YOUR TURN!

1 Create a new e-mail and compose a message to send to two of your group. Send it, copying in two others, one using CC and one using BCC.

2 Create a distribution list for four of your group. Send a second e-mail to everyone on that list.

Attaching files to an e-mail

One of the benefits of e-mail communication is the facility to attach a file to an e-mail.

HOW TO... Attach a file to an e-mail

 1 Create your e-mail, completing all fields as necessary.

 2 Click on the Attach file button in *Yahoo!* or, in *Outlook*, click on the paperclip icon or select Insert/File.

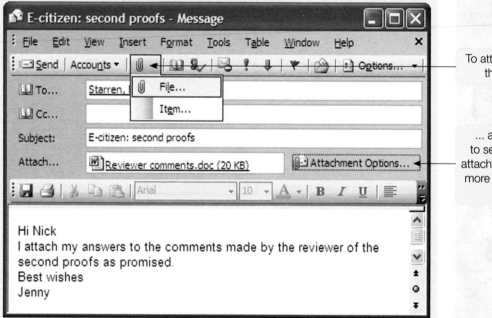

To attach a file, click on the paperclip ...

... and then browse to select the file to be attached. You can attach more than one file to an email.

 3 Browse to locate the file(s) that you want to attach. In *Yahoo!*, you name all the files and attach them in one go. In *Outlook*, each one is attached as you select it.

 4 The file(s) you have attached show on the e-mail form. If you want to change your mind, you can delete an attached file. It does not delete the original file, only the copy that has been created in your Temporary folder, ready to be sent with the e-mail.

YOUR TURN!

1 Check how you will attach a file using your e-mail software.
2 Create a new e-mail. Address it to your tutor, and attach one of the files in your ECDL folder. In the subject line, put the name of the file you have attached.

Replying to and forwarding e-mails

When you receive an e-mail, you might want to reply to it, or to forward it to someone else.

Rather than creatin a new e-mail, you can opt for Reply or Forward; this will save you completing some information in the e-mail form.

The To: and Subject fields are completed automatically when you click on Reply.

You only need to type your reply.

What the incoming e-mail said appears here, so your reply can be very brief.

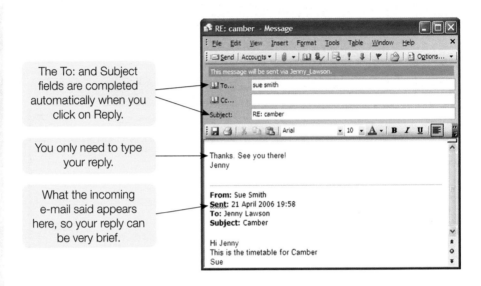

Replying to an e-mail

You have two options: Reply or Reply to all.

* Reply sets up the To field automatically with the name of the person who sent you the e-mail.

* Reply to all sets up the To field to include the sender and everyone else who was sent the e-mail.

The subject line is set up automatically too. 'RE:' is inserted in front of the original subject line.

Forwarding an e-mail

If you select Forward, the To field is not completed for you (because you need to specify the intended recipients). However, the subject line is set up automatically. 'FW:' is inserted in front of the original subject line.

YOUR TURN!

1 For one e-mail in your inbox, reply to the sender, thanking them.

2 For another e-mail, reply to all those listed, saying that you have noted the information.

3 Forward another e-mail to someone in your group. In the message area, write 'FYI'.

Updating your address book

The address book can be used to store e-mail addresses, to save you typing them over and over again.

It can also be used to retain other information about your contacts, such as their telephone numbers and home/business addresses.

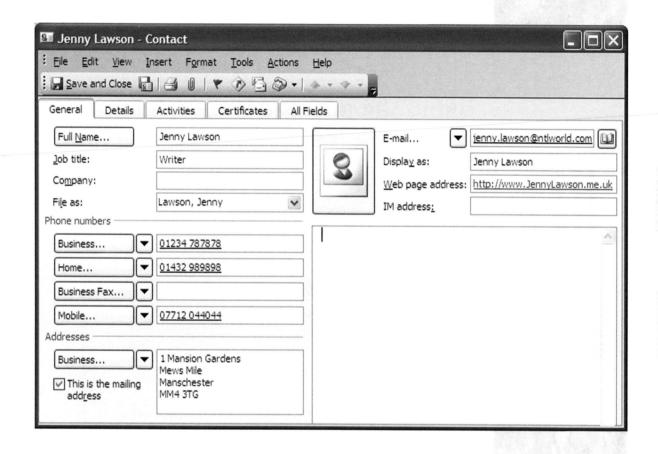

Entering new details into your address book

There are two ways of entering new details into your address book: automatically or manually.

* Each time you receive an e-mail, you can decide whether to add the sender and any other recipients to your address book. This saves you typing the address and reduces the chances of introducing errors.

* You can also enter new details by creating a new contact in your address book. Be very careful to type the e-mail address accurately.

DEMO

Your tutor will show you how to add the e-mail addresses of people who send you e-mails to your address book.

Editing existing entries in your address book

It is important that your address book is kept up to date.

If you receive an e-mail telling you that an e-mail cannot be delivered because the address is not recognised, you should contact the person by some other method (e.g. by telephone) and ask for the correct e-mail address.

Whatever e-mail software you are using, there will be an option to open the contact details for an individual. You can then overwrite the wrong entries with the correct data and click on Save.

Using the address book when creating e-mails

The address book is invaluable for completing the To, CC and BCC fields on the e-mail form.

Most e-mail software, when you start to type a name, will offer possibilities from your address book. Some software offers the option of giving your contacts nicknames to make this process even slicker.

You only have to key one letter and the address is offered.

If several contacts share the same starting letters, the droo-down list will be longer.

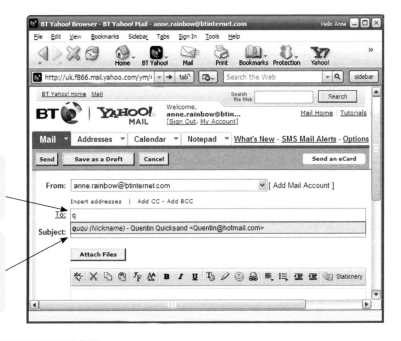

YOUR TURN!

1 For each e-mail in your inbox, consider whether you would like to include the sender and any other recipients in your address book. Add those that you want.

2 Review the entries in your address book. Amend the information to include additional useful information, such as telephone numbers and home addresses.

Record of achievement

Tick the boxes as you work through this course. When you have ticked everything you should be ready to take the examination.

BLOCK 1: Foundation skills

	Done	Revised
THE COMPUTER		
The hardware bits	☐	☐
Turning on your computer	☐	☐
All about icons and menus	☐	☐
All about windows	☐	☐
Using the mouse and keyboard	☐	☐
Shutting down properly	☐	☐
Using Help	☐	☐
FILES AND FOLDERS		
Viewing folders	☐	☐
File types	☐	☐
Copying files and folder	☐	☐
Moving files and folders	☐	☐
Deleting files and folders	☐	☐
SIMPLE APPLICATIONS		
Creating a new document	☐	☐
Opening existing documents	☐	☐
Entering and editing text	☐	☐
Saving files in different formats	☐	☐
Printing	☐	☐
INTERNET BASICS		
What is the Internet?	☐	☐
What is the WWW?	☐	☐
The hardware and software	☐	☐
Web addresses	☐	☐
Using URLs to access web pages	☐	☐
Navigating the Web	☐	☐
E-MAIL BASICS		
What is e-mail?	☐	☐
E-mail addresses	☐	☐
Terminology	☐	☐

	Done	Revised
Creating an e-mail message	☐	☐
Opening an e-mail	☐	☐
Sending an e-mail	☐	☐
Attaching files to an e-mail	☐	☐
Replying to and forwarding e-mails	☐	☐
Updating your address book	☐	☐

Block 2

Information search

In this block, you will become aware of the nature and extent of information on the Internet.

- You will explore nine areas: news, government, consumer, travel, education/training, employment, health, interest groups and business.
- You will learn how to search for information from a wide range of Internet sources using browsing and keyword search techniques.
- You will find out how to retain information found on the Internet, e.g. by copying and pasting it to a document, or saving it in a file.
- You will consider some of the issues and risks associated with using the Internet, such as reliability of information, secure access, viruses, unsolicited e-mail, security of personal data and parental control of web access.
- You will also learn to take precautionary measures when using the Internet.

Lifeskills and benefits from use

When you have completed Block 2 of this course, you should:

* have an appreciation of the breadth and depth of information available in the most used Internet areas such as news, government, consumer, travel, education/training, employment, health, interest groups and business

* be able to browse and search for information effectively

* know how to retain/store information retrieved in a useful format

* appreciate the security risks of using the Internet and be aware of the issues of the reliability and authenticity of the Internet as an information source.

In completing Block 2, you will acquire information search lifeskills that will enable you, as an e-Citizen, to find relevant information that you require in a reliable and confident way. These information search lifeskills will also provide you with a convenient way to access lifelong learning.

Having completed Block 2, you will be ready to tackle the Block 2 questions in the test – and move on to study block 3.

Searching

In this section, you will learn about using your computer and an Internet link to search for information.

What is a search engine?

A search engine is an Internet tool that you can use to search for websites that hold information of interest to you.

There are a number of search engines, and you would be advised to use more than one when doing any kind of research. Each search engine has its strengths and weaknesses, and you might miss something if you restrict your research to just one.

Locating a search engine

The search engines can be found on the Internet! They offer their services via their websites. So, if you know the URL, you can locate the website and then use the search options available.

Many are general-purpose search engines.

Search engines	URL
AltaVista	uk.altavista.com
Ask	uk.ask.com
Google	www.google.co.uk
MSN Search	search.msn.co.uk
Yahoo!	uk.search.yahoo.com

Other search engines focus on particular topics, such as accommodation (www.ase.net), travel (www.aardvarktravel.net) and biker sites (www.bikers-engine.com).

Some websites – such as Search.com and dogpile.co.uk – promise to provide a one-stop search service; this incorporates results from several other search engines such as *Ask*, *Google*, *LookSmart*, *MSN* and *Yahoo!*.

YOUR TURN!

1 Open a new document in *Word* or some other word processing package. Create a table similar to that shown above.
2 With others in your group, share experiences of using search engines, and note the names of the search engines which proved most useful.
3 Extend the table to include search engines of interest to you. Save your file in your ECDL folder as 'Search'.

Using a search engine

A search engine will provide a **hit list** of websites – with their URLs as hyperlinks – in response to a **keyword** supplied by you. So, you decide what keywords to use, enter them in the Search window and press Search (or Go or something similar) and that's it! Well, not quite …

Choosing the best keywords can be tricky:

❋ Suppose you want to hire a boat. Searching on 'boat hire' might give you too many hits to be useful.

❋ Suppose you want to hire a tent to put up in your garden. This could be called a tent, or a gazebo, or a marquee, depending on its size.

You need to be specific, rather than using general words.

The order and spelling of your keywords can also affect your results. A mis-spelling may result in no hits at all.

What does it mean?

HIT LIST
A list of websites that match a criteria, including a hyperlink to each site.

KEYWORD
This word (or phrase) is used by the search engine to identify websites whose content matches it and therefore may be of interest.

Keyword(s) chosen by you.

If you get no hits, choose an alternative keyword.

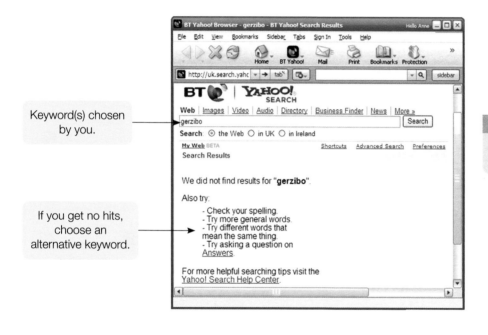

DEMO
Your tutor will show you how to set up a search.

If your choice of keywords results in too few (none!) or too many matching websites, or just not the ones you wanted, you will need to rethink your search.

❋ You may want to change the focus on where you are looking. This could include using a different search engine, or just changing the keywords.

❋ You may need to refine the search and might try to narrow it by combining criteria.

COMBINED CRITERIA
See page 102.

Portal sites

Portals are Internet versions of newspapers or magazines. Just like real daily publications, these portal sites want to grab your attention and keep it for as long as possible.

BOOKMARK
See page 115.

Portals would like you to **bookmark** them, and preferably for you to make them your home page, so that their site is your first stop when you open your browser software and log on to the Internet.

Yahoo! is an example of a consumer portal.

Portal sites such as Yahoo! provide a wide range of services, including free e-mail, personalised home pages, instant messages and chat rooms.

All portal sites are designed for your convenience when on the Internet. Some portals are targeted at specific industries; these are called **vertical portals**.

Others, called **enterprise portals**, are like consumer portals but are designed for large corporations and organisations.

YOUR TURN!

1 Compare notes with others in your group. What portals do you use already?

2 Visit *Yahoo!* (http://uk.yahoo.com) and explore all the services on offer: mail, music, and much more.

Keyword searches

The keyword method of searching using a search engine is very similar to that used when searching for help.

REMEMBER
Help searches are described on page 25-9.

HOW TO... Use a search engine for a keyword search

 1 Open your web browser software.

 2 Log on to the Internet.

 3 Go to your portal site (such as *Yahoo!*), or to a search engine (such as *Google*).

 4 Click on the search window.

 5 Type in your keyword and press Enter, or click on Search, or click on Go (depending on your software).

Enter your keyword(s) here ...

... and click Search.

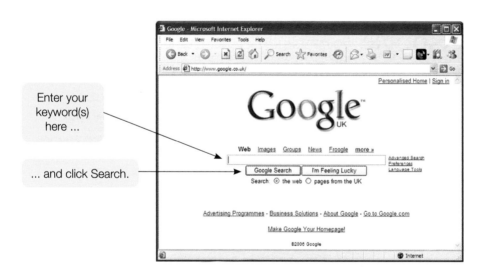

YOUR TURN!

1 For this course, you will explore nine areas: news, government, consumer issues, travel, education/training, employment, health, interest groups and business. For each of these, write four keywords that you might use to search the web. For example, for travel, you might need information on 'Prices' of a 'Ferry' from 'Dover' to 'Calais'.

2 Try out a keyword search using two different search engines but using only one of your keywords, e.g. 'Ferry'. Compare the results. How many hits were there? Which websites appeared in the top five hits for each? What **sponsored links** were offered?

What does it mean?

SPONSORED LINKS
Some websites pay to be included in the hit list for certain keywords.

Combining criteria

A keyword search on 'Ferry' across the whole web returns more than 51 million hits in only 0.14 seconds. This is not very useful, so you need to narrow down the search so as to reduce the number of hits to a more manageable number. Searching instead on 'Prices' and 'Ferry' reduces the hit list to a mere 6 million … but if you reduce it to UK sites only, the number of hits falls dramatically to 1.73 million.

If you narrow the search even more, say, to include 'Dover', the hit list falls to 185,000. Including 'Calais' reduces it to 114,000 hits.

It is most unlikely that you will look at all these websites, but the more you combine criteria, the shorter and maybe more appropriate the hit list becomes.

YOUR TURN!

1 Using the keywords you chose for the 'health' topic, do a search using one, two, three and all four keywords, and compare the number of hits that are returned. Notice the top five sites listed in each case. What is the effect of reordering the keywords?
2 Reduce the scope of the search by opting for UK pages only. What effect does this have?
3 Restart the search, and locate, for example, a health centre close to your home.

> **! HANDY TIP**
> All local councils have a website and provide links to local services for residents.

Advanced search criteria

Using the search window and simply writing a string of keywords is a very clumsy way of searching the web.

There are other options that provide more effective search results.

✳ You can restrict the scope of the search to UK sites only (or, with *Yahoo!*, to Ireland only).

✳ *Yahoo!* offers search shortcuts which list a number of topics (weather, world clock, images …) and examples of the keywords you might use, before you press the Search button.

✳ *Yahoo!* also offers an Advanced Web Search. This involves completing a form to specify as many conditions as are necessary for you.

REMEMBER
You completed an onscreen form when creating a new e-mail message; see page 84.

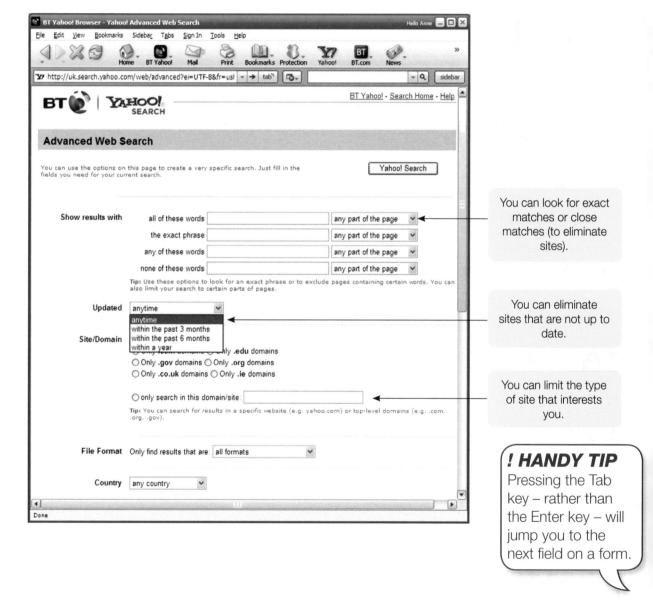

You can look for exact matches or close matches (to eliminate sites).

You can eliminate sites that are not up to date.

You can limit the type of site that interests you.

! HANDY TIP
Pressing the Tab key – rather than the Enter key – will jump you to the next field on a form.

Yahoo! is not the only portal to offer advanced search features. Other portals and search engines offer similar options, and it is important that you explore these. In alphabetical order, here are some suggestions as to what is available.

❋ *AltaVista* has an advanced form you can complete, and their search button is labelled FIND.

❋ *Ask* has a user-friendly interface with sections that lead to relevant forms for you to complete.

❋ *Dogpile* says it has 'all the best search engines piled into one' and refers to *Google, Yahoo!, MSN* and *Ask*. It promotes itself as a fun site – and includes a Joke of the Day. Its Search button is labelled 'Go Fetch!'.

❋ *MSN* offers Advanced options through a Search Builder.

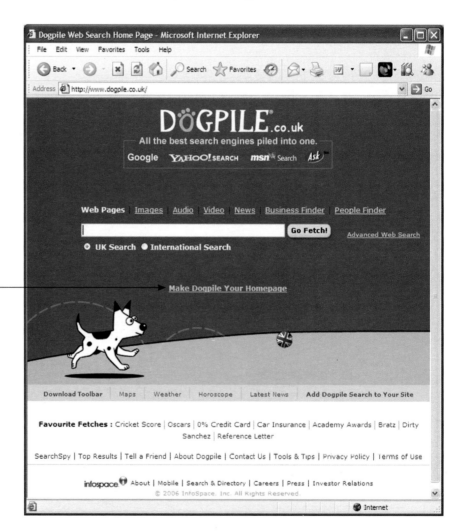

Notice that you can make this your home page by clicking here.

DEMO

Your tutor will show you how to download a toolbar.

YOUR TURN!

1 Explore some search engine sites and try them out using an advanced search. Compare the results.

2 *Google* and *Yahoo!* both offer a toolbar which provides a search window on your screen at all times. Look at these and discuss with others in your group how useful this feature might be.

Searching by navigating

Having found the right website, you may have to dig a little deeper to find exactly what you seek, using hyperlinks: text links (below) and image links (page 106).

Navigating your way using text links

The BBC website offers the option to listen to recordings of programmes that have been broadcast recently.

To locate the programme that you want to listen to, you need to navigate your way through the BBC website.

HOW TO... **Navigate through the BBC site**

 1 If you don't know the URL for the BBC site, and don't have a link in your History folder, try BBC as a search word in *Google* and click on the 'I'm feeling lucky!' button.

 2 Study the BBC's home page to see what is on offer. Look in particular for the section of the home page that refers to radio, and look for a message that says 'Listen to shows you've missed'.

 3 Look for the text link. The word 'Listen' is in bold and if you roll your cursor over the sentence the text becomes underlined, indicating that it is a link, and the cursor changes to a pointing finger.

 4 Clicking on this link opens a new window: the BBC Radio Player. Notice that there are also tabs at the top of the panel, e.g. NEWS PLAYER and SPORT PLAYER.

 5 All the radio stations listed, and the types of show, and the speech options are links. Click on Soap.

 6 Locate *The Archers* – and select an episode from two or three days ago. You needn't listen to it!

 7 Close the Radio Player window to go back to the BBC home page.

REMEMBER
The History folder lists all websites you have visited recently (page 70).

! HANDY TIP
When your cursor is on a link, its URL is displayed in the bottom left of the browser window.

Navigating your way using image links

REMEMBER
The pointer – or cursor – can change shape as you move the mouse. This indicates what you can do with an object that the cursor is on or near.

Some websites provide images as the hyperlinks to the next page. Typically, these websites have products to sell, and you are encouraged to click on the image of a product to learn more about it.

✴ If you move your mouse across your mouse mat so that the pointer moves across images or potential text links, you may see a change in the appearance of the pointer. This can indicate a link.

✴ The pointer may change shape from an arrow to a pointing finger.

✴ A URL may be displayed in the bottom left corner of your browser window.

A hand with a pointing finger is the standard pointer icon for a hyperlink.

YOUR TURN!

1 Visit the website of the office supplier Mr Office **(www.mr-office.com/).** Navigate through this site, using image links to find out the cost of a ream of photocopying paper.

2 Visit the Amazon website (guess the URL, or use a search engine to locate it). Go to the Music section and use image links to find out more about one of the new and future releases.

Searching and browsing

If you know the name of the organisation whose site you think will provide the information you need, you could simply go to their website by typing the URL of the website in the browser address bar.

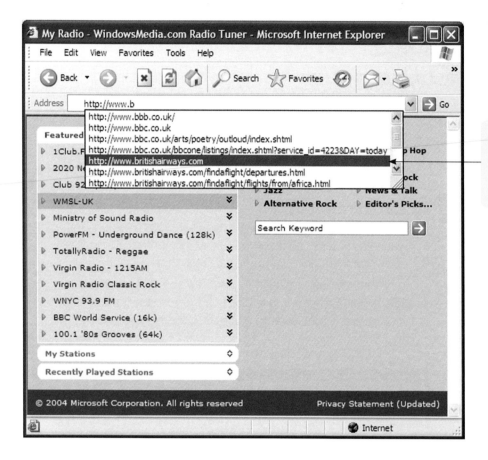

If you know which page in a website you need, you can save yourself time by selecting a longer URL.

Some sites also provide links to other sites. So if, when you reach a site, it does not seem to provide what you want, check the menu bar for signs to Useful Links.

YOUR TURN!

1 Open your browser, and visit a site you have visited previously by entering the beginning of the URL in the address bar and then selecting from the drop-down list offered.

2 Once on the site, browse through it to find useful links to other sites. Visit those sites, and from them go on to visit other useful sites. Use your Back button to return to the original site.

Using Copy in a browser window

Once you have located the information that is of interest to you, you may want to copy some of the material from the web page.

⚠ WARNING! Make sure you have permission to copy material before doing so. See copyright legislation on page 110.

HOW TO... Copy text in a browser window

 1 Highlight the material by clicking the mouse at the start and dragging the mouse to highlight the text that interests you, and then release the mouse.

 2 With the cursor on the highlighted text, right-click to reveal the context-sensitive menu and select Copy (or use the shortcut key: Ctrl-C). This copies the text you have highlighted on to the clipboard.

 3 You could then paste the clipboard contents into a Word document, for example, but it may not work if the original text was in a table, or had some special formatting. So, instead, open *Notepad* and paste the text into that.

 4 In *Notepad*, use the shortcut key Ctrl-A to select all the text (or select Edit/Select All), and then Ctrl-C to copy it back to the clipboard (or right-click to reveal the context-sensitive menu and select Copy).

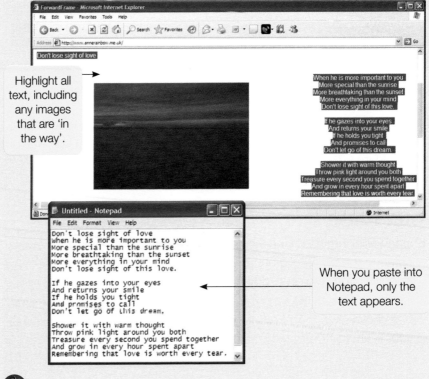

Highlight all text, including any images that are 'in the way'.

When you paste into Notepad, only the text appears.

 5 Now paste the text into a Word document.

Saving an image from a web page

If you plan to copy an image from a web page (having first obtained permission), you can simply right-click on it and use Copy to put it on the clipboard.

However, if you are looking for suitable images, and/or are not ready to paste the image into a document, or might want to use it more than once, you could consider saving the image in a file by itself.

Saving an image using Save As

Depending on your planned use for the image, you might consider saving it as a separate file first, and then inserting the image from that file into your document. Rather than selecting Copy from the context-sensitive menu, select Save Picture As instead.

Select Save Picture As, rather than Copy.

YOUR TURN!

1 Go a website that you have visited before and select some text for copying: text that currently appears within a table. Copy the text using whichever method you prefer, and then paste it into a new *Notepad* document. Also paste it straight into a new Word document. From the *Notepad* version, copy it once more and paste into the same Word document. Compare the two within the Word document.

2 Copy and paste an image from a web page into the Word document. Save the same image on the site in your ECDL folder and then use Insert/Picture to insert it into the Word document. Compare the two.

> **! HANDY TIP**
> You may copy the URL from a web page and paste it into an e-mail to send it to a friend. They can then click on the link and go to the web page.

Copyright legislation

Legislation exists to protect originators of written words and images that you may find on a website. So, there are restrictions on copying – and using – material from a website with which you must comply. To check what is protected, look for the copyright symbol (©) on the website.

Please do not copy the text of the poems or stories on this site. If you wish to include material in a publication, please apply to Anne Rainbow for permission.

The photos on this site are reproduced with the kind permission of the appropriate copyright holders. Copying any of these photos is not permitted without the express permission of the individual copyright holder. Relevant links are provided on each page so that you can make contact with the photographer if you so wish.

This site was last updated on 6 April 2006

Sketch: Stevie Roberts 2004

© Text: Anne Rainbow 2005

Email Anne at anne.rainbow@btinternet.com

 WARNING!
Make sure that you obtain permission before you reproduce material, and that, having been given permission, you acknowledge your source as required by the copyright holder.

Copied material – accepted codes

If you do decide to copy material and use it in your own work, you should include an acknowledgement of the source (which will help your reader to trace it back to your sources if they want), and to have paid any amount required for permission to be granted for its reproduction.

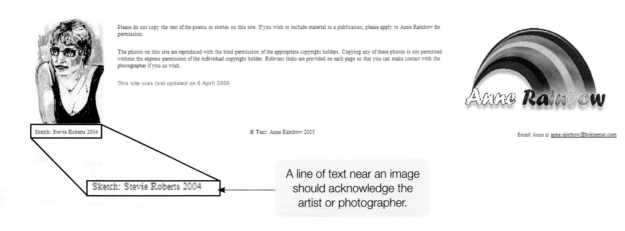

A line of text near an image should acknowledge the artist or photographer.

YOUR TURN!

1 Search the Internet for information about copyright legislation. What is meant by intellectual property? For how long does copyright apply?

2 In *Word*, search Help to find out how to insert the copyright symbol into a word processed document.

Saving a web page

Having found a web page that interests you, you might want to save a copy of it on your hard disk, or on to a CD, or on to a floppy disk. You have several options:

* You can make a copy of the web page as it is and save this somewhere on your computer: on the hard disk, on a CD, or on a floppy disk.

* You can make a page available offline, and have the option of having it updated regularly.

Making pages available for offline viewing

This would mean you could read its content when your computer is not connected to the Internet.

DEMO
Your tutor will show you how to save a web page to disk.

HOW TO... **Make the current page available offline**

 1 On the Favorites menu, click Add to Favorites.

 2 Tick the Make available offline box.

DEMO
Your tutor will show you how to make the current page available offline.

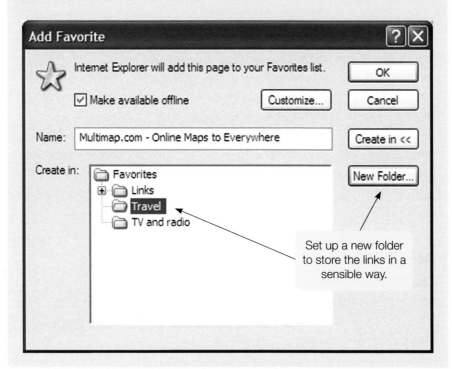

You can arrange for the page to be updated when you are next online if necessary; otherwise, what you see would be the one saved that particular day.

Copying a web page to the hard drive

You can save a web page to your hard drive – or to a CD or floppy disk – through File/Save As.

✳ If you want the whole page, including all images, opt for Web Page Complete. The HTML file plus any associated images will be saved as a folder in a folder location of your choosing. The HTML file will automatically open in a browser when you double-click on it.

✳ An alternative is HTML only – this does not save graphics and sounds, so only the one file is created. If you double-click on this one, all the images will appear as rectangles with a small red cross – there are no images saved, only the text.

✳ You can also opt for Text only, which means you will lose any formatting. This file is saved with a .txt file extension and can be opened in a text editor such as *Notepad*.

Which method you choose is determined by what you plan to do with the copied material.

YOUR TURN!

1 Make a web page available offline.
2 Save a copy of a complete web page in your ECDL folder.
3 Save a copy of the HTML for the same web page in your ECDL folder.
4 Save a copy of the same web page, as text only.
5 Examine the directory of your ECDL folder to identify how these copies have been saved. What file extensions have been used?
6 Open each one to compare what material is available to you.

Printing a web page

If you click on the **print icon** on the browser toolbar, you will send a copy of the whole web page to your printer. However, this may not give you what you want!

✳ Sometimes, if you click on the print icon, parts of the page – probably the right-hand side of the image – are lost in the transfer.

✳ Some web pages are very long, and you could print several pages of material that you do not need, wasting paper and ink.

You can check what will be printed by selecting File/**Print Preview**.

✳ It may be that changing the **page setup** to print in landscape orientation will allow the full width of the web page to be printed, although it is then even more likely to run on to more than one page.

✳ It may also be more effective to copy and paste material into a word processed document, and to print from there.

So, first you must decide what it is you want to print. Look carefully at the web page to identify exactly what you need.

Printing a selection from a web page

If you don't need the whole page, you can print a selection, which includes some text and maybe some images.

PRINT ICON
See page 14.

PRINT PREVIEW ICON
See page 14.

PAGE SETUP
See page 56.

REMEMBER
Landscape is with the long side at the top; see page 56.

HOW TO... **Print a selection from a web page**

 1 Use drag to highlight the material you want to print.

 2 Right-click and select Print.

 3 On the Print dialogue box, click Selection.

 4 Click OK.

DEMO
Your tutor will show you how to print a selection.

Printer-friendly option

Some websites, such as Multimap, offer a printer-friendly version for material that they expect you to want to print. Clicking on the link opens a new window, and what is shown in that window will print as is, just how you need it.

What does it mean?

ZOOM IN
To magnify an image in order to show more detail.

YOUR TURN!

1 Visit the Multimap website (www.multimap.com). Enter your own postcode in the Search field. **Zoom in** and out until you have a view which shows the nearest railway station to your home. Opt for the printer-friendly format and print one copy.

When you roll the cursor across the printer icon, you are invited to view a printer-friendly version of the map.

2 Copy the image – you are authorised to make one copy of the map image on the page for personal use – and save it in your ECDL folder.

3 Create a new word processed document which explains how to reach your home and includes the map.

Bookmarking a favourite web page

If you visit a website and would like the option to return, you need to make a note of the URL.

One way is to create a **bookmark**, so that you add the URL to your **Favorites** folder.

HOW TO... **Create a bookmark**

 1 Go the web page you want to bookmark. Make sure it has fully downloaded.

 2 In *Yahoo!*, click on the Bookmark icon. Click on Add. The link is added to your list of favorites. You can then edit your link and create folders to manage your links.

 3 In *Internet Explorer*, to open the Favorites panel, click on the Favorites icon. On the Favorites panel, click on Add. You can browse to decide where in your Favorites folder you would like the link to be stored. If you want to, you may create a new folder for this link. You can also decide a name for the link, before it is added to your list of favorites. You can also edit your bookmarks at a later date.

YOUR TURN!

1 Use your History folder to return to the sites you have visited recently. Make bookmarks for those you think you will need to visit in the future.

2 For each of the nine areas of research (news, government, consumer issues, travel, education and training, employment, health, interest groups and business) locate (using a search engine if you wish) and bookmark at least one relevant site.

3 Find out how to control how far back your History folder remembers URLs, and change this setting.

What does it mean?

BOOKMARK
A URL remembered in your Favorites folder.

What does it mean?

FAVORITES
This folder is used to hold all bookmarks, i.e. links to websites, that you may want to revisit.

 Favorites

> **REMEMBER**
> You can search Help to find out how to do things.

Precautions

In this section, the focus in on how searching the Internet and using e-mail can bring exposure to electronic junk mail, computer viruses and content that you might find inappropriate or offensive. You will learn how to take precautions to protect your computer from electronic threats.

Internet exposure to risks

Searching the Internet and using e-mail can bring exposure to junk mail, computer viruses and content that you might find inappropriate or offensive.

Risks when connected to the Internet

All Internet services have an associated **port** number to connect to when making an Internet connection. For example, the WWW usually uses port number 80, and mail uses port number 23. So, when your computer is linked to the Internet, ports on your computer are opened to let the information flow to and fro.

Most of this information flow is intentional and harmless:

* E-mails are sent from your outbox, and others come into your inbox.
* Each time you ask your browser, a request is sent and a web page is downloaded into your Temporary folder.
* If you register your software, such as your word processing program, the software provider may regularly attempt to check whether you have the most up-to-date version of the software.
* If you install a virus checker, the software may be programmed to automatically download the latest DAT files when new viruses are discovered.

However, some flow of information may be undesirable.

* Junk mail that can arrive with your legitimate mail may include viruses and present a risk to your data.
* The variety of information on the web may expose you to material that you would rather not see, so pages that can be downloaded may need to be controlled.

This section considers both issues.

How to deal with junk mail

Junk mail is unsolicited mail. You can do nothing to stop the person who sends it from doing so, but you can reduce the irritation of junk mail by following two simple procedures.

* Install a **spam filter** to place mail that is suspect in a separate inbox: *Norton* call this the *Norton Antispam* folder; *Yahoo!* calls theirs your Bulk folder – mainly because, if you are a recipient in a **bulk mailing**, it will land in the Bulk folder first.
* Delete e-mails, without reading them, if they are from someone or some organisation you do not recognise. Reading junk mail can raise stress levels; judicious use of the Delete key can reduce them!

What does it mean?

PORT
An entry (or departure) point for data – and maybe hackers and viruses.

REMEMBER
DAT files contain the profile of a virus, including its signature; see page 82.

SPAM FILTER
See page 80.

What does it mean?

BULK MAILING
The same e-mail message sent to many recipients.

Range of information on the Internet

The Internet gives you access to the WWW, and to all web pages that are on offer.

* Some are created by organisations that take care not to publish material that will offend you.
* Others focus on topics that are of interest to some, but may be highly offensive to you.

To avoid being confronted with such sites, or younger viewers stumbling across them, you can set up controls to limit the sites that can be viewed on your computer. This acts as a filter, and is explained further on page 129.

YOUR TURN!

1 Use Help to find out how to delete an e-mail in your inbox without reading it. If the deleted mail goes into a Deleted Mail folder, find out how to empty it.
2 Use Help to find out how to use an online calendar to set up a reminder to check your Bulk inbox. Set up the reminder to remind you once a week.

DEMO

Your tutor will show you how to set up an online calendar, and how to use it to remind yourself to do things.

What does it mean?

VIRUS
A program that can cause damage to the data on a computer.

REBOOT
Close down and restart.

CRASH
The screen freezes and clicking the mouse or pressing keys on the keyboard has no effect.

Viruses

Computer **viruses** show themselves in various ways.

* Your computer may spontaneously **reboot** or your system or its applications may **crash**.
* You may experience problems with sound: e.g. no sound! Or you may see screen display anomalies such as distortion, misshapen images, or missing video.
* You may 'lose' files or files may no longer open. Or your CD drive may not function.

Any such 'strange' behaviour can indicate a virus attack, and should be investigated before the virus can do more damage or transfer to other computers.

How viruses are contracted

A computer virus is man-made and is often disguised as a game or image with a title that might encourage you to open it.

The Melissa virus was created to affect *Word 97* and *Word 2000* documents. It opened *Microsoft Outlook* and sent itself to 50 people in *Outlook's* address book. The subject line read 'Important message from [you!]' and the message read: 'Here is the document you asked for ... don't show anyone else.'

Of course, many people did not recognise this as a virus and they opened it. Having done so, they were infected.

Then, another 50 e-mails from each infected computer were sent out; so, in no time at all, this virus had spread worldwide. Apart from the volume of e-mail traffic created, which slowed down the Internet for genuine users, the virus also corrupted *Word* documents that were opened at a specific time by inserting the text 'Twenty-two points, plus triple-word-score, plus fifty points for using all my letters. Game's over. I'm outta here.'

Anti-virus software

Protection against virus attack is available in the form of anti-virus software.

This software – from organisations such as *Norton* and *McAfee* – relies on access to the most up-to-date information on virus threats and is therefore only available on subscription. This means you buy the right to have it installed on your computer and will receive updates (automatically if you wish) so that you are as protected as you can be at any moment. However, the subscription lasts for a limited time, and then you need to renew it – i.e. pay again!

Types of virus checker

There are several different types of virus checker product available, so your system can be protected in a variety of ways.

❋ **Virus scanner software** is the most common form of anti-virus software. The scan is initiated by the user, but you can automate this and schedule the scan to take place at regular intervals.

❋ **Start-up virus scanner software** runs each time the PC is booted up. It checks only for **boot sector viruses**.

BOOT SECTOR VIRUS See page 120.

❋ **Memory-resident virus scanner software** stays in memory and checks incoming e-mails and browser documents, and so automatically checks the environment in which your PC operates.

❋ A **behaviour-based detector** is a form of memory-resident virus scanner software that watches for behaviour that would indicate the presence of a virus.

All of these provide protection. While the memory-resident virus scanner software gives adequate reassurance to most users that they are protected, other scans are needed too.

	Types of virus
Imposter virus	An e-mail warning of a virus suggests that you check whether you have a particular file on your hard disk. When you check, you find that you do have this file and set about deleting the offending file as per instructions given in the e-mail, only to find that it was a hoax. Apart from the waste of time, and the stress involved in thinking you have a virus, you may accidentally delete an important file and reduce the functionality of your PC software.
Boot sector virus	This plants itself in the **boot sector** of every bootable floppy disk or hard disk, guaranteeing that it will run each time you boot up. These viruses spread from disk to disk, and hence from PC to PC if you take a floppy disk from one PC to another.
File viruses	These are infected program files with extensions of .exe or .com. When the program is run, it does what damage it is designed to do.
Macro viruses	These hide within the macros of applications such as *Word*, and are spread from one open document to another.
BIOS viruses	These attack the **flash BIOS**, overwriting the system BIOS and making the PC unbootable.
Trojan horse	It infiltrates a PC by pretending to be a file or program that would normally be found on a PC. It takes its name from the Greek myth in which a gift of a huge wooden horse was a ruse to smuggle soldiers, hidden within the horse, inside the city walls of Troy. When executed, the Trojan horse program tends to compromise the PC's security. It can also slow down a system and cause it to crash.
Worm or e-mail virus	A worm can send on e-mails – and the virus – to all your contacts using data from your address book. It tends to create a spoof message which might fool someone who receives the e-mail into thinking it is genuinely from the sender.

Virus checker software

If your computer is behaving strangely and you suspect a virus, you should scan your hard disk and any other storage devices. However, your computer may seem fine and you may still have a virus – one that could cause problems at a later date. So, it is important to check regularly for viruses, even when things seem to be OK.

You could make a mental note to do this every Thursday morning, for example, but a better option might be to create a **scheduled task**, so that it happens automatically on a regular basis.

REMEMBER
You know how to do a virus scan; see page 83.

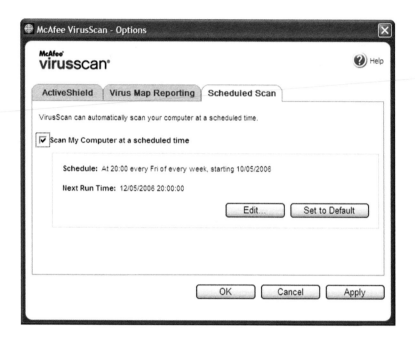

Memory-resident virus checker

Although the memory-resident virus checker gives peace of mind, it may also interrupt you, e.g. when sending out e-mails.

If several consecutive e-mails look too similar, the anti-virus software suspects that a worm may be at work. It therefore questions you, and you have to decide whether to send the e-mail message.

Often, you will want to, because the e-mails are genuine.

Don't be tempted to turn off the virus scanner when you send out lots of similar e-mails and it keeps making you confirm your intention. Better to be interrupted, even a lot, than to be infected!

YOUR TURN!

1 Find out how to set up a virus scan as a scheduled task within your virus-checker software.
2 Send several identical e-mails to see what happens.

Securing personal data

There are lots of situations where you will be asked for personal data while on the Internet.

* It is possible to do all your banking online: paying bills, moving money to and from savings accounts, and printing statements.

* You can file your tax return online, supplying details of your earnings and expenses.

* Service suppliers like BT and the gas and electricity companies offer the options to see statements, give readings and change details such as address or telephone number.

* Organisations like insurance companies accept enquiries on the Internet and will expect you to complete a form giving personal details that will allow them to arrive at a quotation for you.

Access to each of your accounts will be via an account number (or customer ID) and a password. Your account number will appear on correspondence and is not 'secret' as such, but it is important to keep your **password** secret.

What does it mean?

PASSWORD
A secret string of characters (letters and digits) used to gain access to private data or programs.

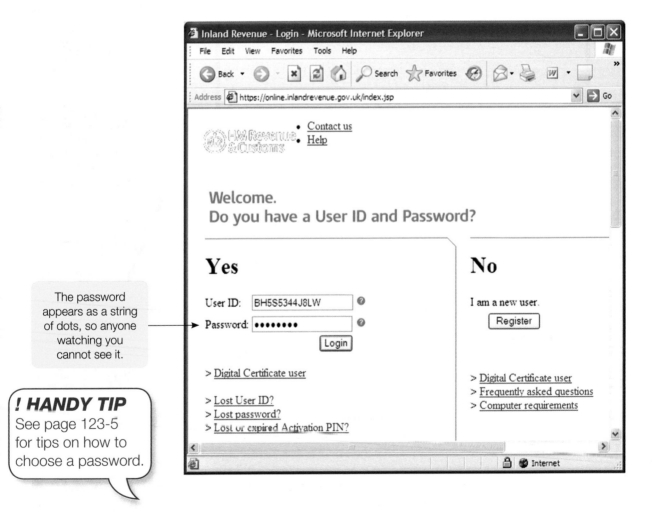

The password appears as a string of dots, so anyone watching you cannot see it.

! HANDY TIP
See page 123-5 for tips on how to choose a password.

Passwords

Choosing a password is a bit of a balancing act: you need something that is easy for you to remember and yet difficult for someone else to guess. The tables of DOs (page 124-5) and DON'Ts show how best to choose a password and keep it safe.

Password DON'Ts	
DON'T … share it	Your password gives entry to an account that is assigned to you. You will be held responsible for the activities of the account.
DON'T … write it down	Passwords that are written down can be seen and stolen.
DON'T … store it in a program	Many e-mail clients, web browsers, and web services offer to store your password to save you having to type it in each time. This is a bad idea, because it is easy for hackers to recover your password from inside one of these programs if they have access to your computer (and sometimes even if they don't). Some computer viruses may also be able to recover your password from such stores and e-mail them to random people or post them publicly on the Internet.
DON'T … use dictionary words	One method of guessing passwords is to use a **brute force attack**. All words found in online dictionaries, even foreign dictionaries, can be systematically tried, until the right password is found.
DON'T … use common misspellings	Even replacing 'l' with a '1' does not help. There are dictionaries of commonly misspelt words (called **cracker dictionaries**), so if yours is one of them it can still be discovered.
DON'T … use real names	As with dictionary words, these can be discovered using a brute force attack.
DON'T … use the name of the computer or your account	This would be a first guess for a potential hacker. Even if you reverse it, capitalise alternate letters, or double some letters, this is an easy one to crack systematically.
DON'T … choose something personal	Avoid including personal dates (of birth, anniversaries), special numbers (age, phone number, passport number) or names of nearest and dearest (people, pets, football teams). They are too easy to guess for someone who knows you.

What does it mean?

BRUTE FORCE ATTACK
When a hacker tries all possible passwords until one allows access to the account.

Password DON'Ts continued	
DON'T ... use obvious passwords	Words such as PASS, LETMEIN, OPENSESAME, TEST and number sequences such as 123456 are too easy for a hacker to guess.
DON'T ... use all the same letter or number	AAAAAAA for 7-character code would be so easy to check for! It would be very easy for password cracking software to find this one.
DON'T ... use a pattern on the keyboard	Be aware that you might be watched while keying in your password. So, a password such as QWERTY would be very easy for someone to notice and remember.

Password DOs	
DO ... use as many characters as are allowed	The longer the password, the more difficult it could be to guess. Each additional character increases the total number of combinations possible. A long but relatively simple password can be more secure than a short and complex one, and could be easier to remember.
DO ... use multiple character classes	Most password systems are case sensitive, so including upper and lower cases complicates the password without making it less memorable for you. Include also digits and punctuation marks so that you avoid dictionary terms.
DO ... use letters from a phrase or lyric	Choose a memorable phrase such as 'A bookshop at 84 Charing Cross Rd'. Select letters and digits from it: Ab@84CXR. If you can remember the phrase, you can remember the password and yet it is difficult for someone else to guess. This is sometimes called the **licence plate rule** – creating something you might put on a vanity licence plate.
DO ... invent a pronounceable nonsense word	Consider how words are abbreviated in text messaging and choose something along the same lines: Cul8rAxx.
DO ... substitute or omit letters	You could take a memorable word or phrase like 'MyBakedPotatoes' and lose the vowels: 'MyBkdPtts'.Or use numbers instead of letters: 'Potato' could become 'P0t8t0'. Or use shifted numbers: ! instead of 1, $ instead of 4 and so on. So long as you remember to hold the Shift key down while pressing the digit keys, this part of your password might be easier to remember.

Password DOs continued	
DO ... code using your phone keypad	A phone keypad groups numbers and letters: 1, 2abc, 3def, 4ghi, 5jkl, 6mno, 7pqrs, 8tuv, 9wxyz. If you choose a word or phrase that is memorable to you, such as 'toenail', you can recode that to the first letter of the keypad: 'tmdmagj'. No one could guess it, but if you look at your keypad, you can 'spell' out the word quite easily.

When invited to assign a password to an account, you are asked to enter it twice. This is to make sure that the version you key first – which you cannot read because it is displayed as asterisks – is what you really want.

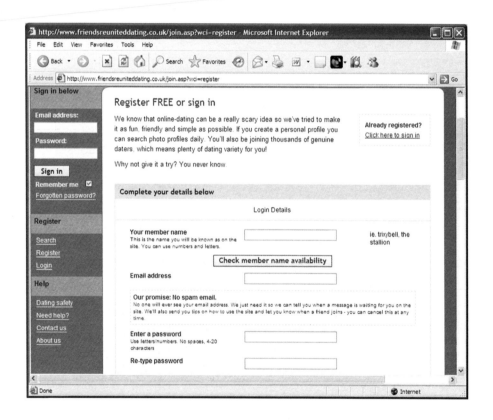

If, having assigned a password, you forget it, most organisations offer to e-mail it to you. This only delays your access to the account, and will provide a written reminder of the access password. If you were to file this e-mail, you could track it down another time, if you were to forget the password again. This makes sense for non-sensitive accounts, especially those that you access infrequently.

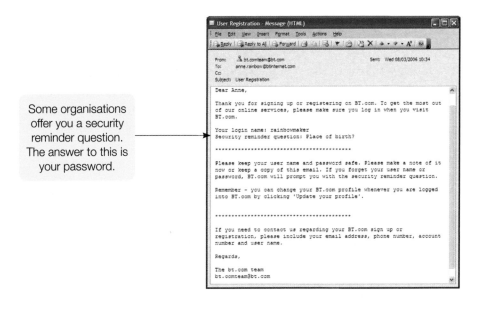

Some organisations offer you a security reminder question. The answer to this is your password.

Identifying secure areas

When entering personal data on the Internet, you run the risk of others – hackers – gaining access to this information and using it to their advantage – and to your disadvantage.

You can be assured of a higher degree of protection on sites that use the **https protocol**. This is because instead of using plain text socket communication as usual, via port 80, the data that is transmitted is encrypted using special protocols, via a different port (usually 443). This ensures reasonable protection from eavesdroppers and attacks by hackers.

There are signs that you are on a secure link:

❋ The URL (in the address bar) starts with the protocol HTTPS.

❋ A locked padlock icon or an unbroken key icon may be displayed in the browser status bar (bottom right-hand corner).

When you leave a secure site, you may be warned.

YOUR TURN!

1 Review the passwords that you use. Change any that you now think might be too easy to guess.

2 Visit the wikipedia site at http://en.wikipedia.org/wiki/HTTPS to learn more about the HTTPS protocol. In particular, read the caveats. Notice how a different coloured font indicates a hyperlink. For any terms that you don't understand, click on the link.

3 Refer to a recent telephone bill (landline or mobile) and look for the web address of your provider.

4 Visit the site and find out how to access your account details.

Consumer rights

There are regulations, set up by the government, which aim to protect the interests of consumers.

For example, businesses are required to disclose detailed information about products, particularly in areas where safety or public health is an issue. So, for example, there are regulations for food labelling.

Consumer protection

Consumer protection recognises that consumers have rights, and consumer organisations exist to help consumers make the best decisions when presented with choices.

CONSUMER RIGHTS
See page 197.

When you purchase goods or services online, you have rights and should be aware of these. They are similar to those you have when purchasing goods or services in a high street shop. However, purchasing on the Internet has resulted in a review of how electronic purchasing might go wrong for the consumer, and new regulations have been introduced to help protect the consumer.

Security of financial transactions

You should expect security of the transactions when you make purchases online. The **HTTPS protocol** goes some way to making transactions more secure, but responsibility also lies with the organisation that collects your personal data to keep this safe.

HTTPS PROTOCOL
See page 126.

YOUR TURN!

1 With others in your group, discuss your experiences of buying goods and services online. What went well? What went wrong?
2 Search the Internet for consumer information sites such as the Citizens Advice Bureau. Bookmark one or more of these sites.

REMEMBER
Bookmarking a site adds its URL to your Favorites folder; see page 115.

Website integrity

In much the same way that you might think twice about buying an apparently expensive watch from a street trader, you need to use your common sense when buying goods or services on the Internet.

Don't assume that every site on the WWW is bona fide. It is relatively easy to set up a website, offer some product that is too good to be true, and then accept monies without providing what has been bought.

So, as with any purchase, make time to find out who you are buying from and deal only with those you consider to be reputable.

Secure access for paying bills

If you want to buy something online and this involves paying online, you may be offered a variety of payment methods.

✳ Paying using your credit card will involve disclosing your credit card number, and most probably the 3-digit code on the reverse side of the card. Although the link may be secure, the data may be held by the vendor and accessed there by hackers, so there is an element of risk, although it should be small.

✳ PayPal and WorldPay are recognised, secure methods of paying and many sites offer this route.

However you buy goods, there is a risk.

✳ If you fill your wallet with £20 notes and go to a store, you might be robbed and lose your cash.

✳ If you pay by credit card in a store, you run similar risks of **identity theft** as you do when buying online.

Buying online offers the benefits of convenience which, perhaps, outweigh any additional risks involved.

Online banking

Online banking has revolutionised the way people handle their finances.

It is now possible to view the state of each current and savings account, to transfer money between accounts instantaneously, to arrange to pay bills and set up standing orders, and to change personal details such as your address, telephone number and e-mail address.

Because this data is so sensitive, banks tend to have additional security checks before you gain access to your data.

For example, Barclays have a customer number (like 20105983654), a security number (like 432199) and a secret word (like GARDEN) from which you have to give two letters.

The method of entering these codes is also becoming more sophisticated. Instead of keying in your password, you select from a drop-down list of letters, using the mouse. This makes it harder for keyloggers to track what you are entering and thus makes the site more secure.

YOUR TURN!

1 Visit the PayPal site, and compare what it offers with WorldPay. (Either guess their URLs, or use a search engine to find them.)

2 Visit a site which offers products for sale. Find out what payment methods they offer.

3 Visit the website of your bank. Notice the protocol being used (HTTP or HTTPS). If you have not yet registered for online banking, consider doing so now. Explore the options available to you, and notice the security arrangements.

4 Visit the site of a credit card company. See what facilities they offer, and what security is in place.

Parental controls

Some material on the WWW would offend some adults and, certainly, there is much that a parent would not want their child to be viewing.

To help parents exercise a level of control over what websites are accessed by their offspring, a range of parental control options are made available by ISPs.

Why restrictions might be set up

Children might normally use the computer under supervision, but there may be occasions when an older child is left to babysit, and the temptation is there to explore 'naughty' material on the web.

Because search engines return a hit list very quickly, a search on, for example, 'boob' could expose a child to as many as 45 million sites, while 'porn' leads to 450 million sites. So, unless a parent trusts the child implicitly, it makes sense to set up controls.

Setting up parental controls: browsers

Parental controls are provided within browser software in much the same way as you can block your children dialling certain numbers from a telephone handset.

For example, *Microsoft Internet Explorer* has a Content Adviser facility which is password protected – so the parent can control it and the child cannot!

Sites (most but not all) are rated according to content in each of four areas: language, nudity, sex and violence. The acceptable ratings can be set up for each user on a computer, to match their age and sensibilities. It is possible to set up a list of websites that are barred, regardless of how each site's content is rated. Similarly, you can set up a list of websites that other people can always view, regardless of how the sites' contents are rated.

Setting up parental controls: messaging

Instant messaging, for example using *Messenger*, can include audio and video links. This software presents opportunities for children to be 'groomed' but the software vendors include a range of controls for parents to minimise such risk.

✳ You can block messages from specific people, and block messages from people you don't know.

✳ You can control whom your child talks to, by monitoring your child's use of *Messenger*.

DEMO
Your tutor will show you how to set up controls.

DEMO
Your tutor will show you the web access options after controls have been set up.

DEMO
Your tutor will show you how to block messages, monitor conversations and obtain an online activity report.

* You can also request an online activity report to see how much time your child spends using *Messenger* and to whom your child talks.

A child, knowing that such controls are in place, is less likely to come to harm.

YOUR TURN!

1 Investigate the web to discover how individual sites are rated in the areas of language, nudity, sex and violence.

2 Check what facilities your web browser offers by way of parental controls. Compare this with others in your group. You may want to consider changing your browser in the light of the parental controls on offer.

3 Experiment with changing the settings, and find out how your web browser blocks or unblocks access to certain sites.

4 Check that you understand how to control access for different individuals on your computer. This may involve setting up separate user areas and user access.

5 Check what control you have over conversations that take place in software like *Messenger*.

6 Discuss how you plan to control access with those that may be affected, e.g. your children.

7 The Internet Watch Foundation (www.iwf.org.uk) runs the UK hotline for reporting illegal content, specifically child abuse images hosted worldwide and criminally obscene and incitement to racial hatred content hosted in the UK. Visit the site to find out what can be done to make the Internet a safer place for children.

DEMO

Your tutor will show you how to set up a new user and to control access for that user.

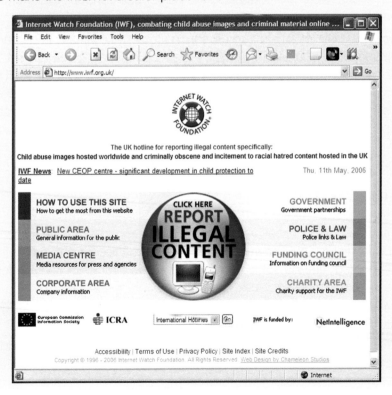

Information

In this section, you will learn about information sources and available online services. You will learn how to browse the web to find information and how to extract useful information in a number of areas. Nine areas are explored but, in the tests, you will only be required to extract information from three selected areas.

News

Because pages on the WWW can be updated so easily, it is the ideal medium for news.

Newspapers still exist in paper form, but more and more people use the Internet to find out what is going on in the world. News via the Internet is available to anyone who has a computer, and the 'newspaper' can include media such as music or video. You have lots of options:

✴ You can access news through sites run by newspaper publishers, such as *The Times* or *The Independent*. Most international, national and local newspapers offer web versions of the hardcopy paper.

✴ You can also learn about breaking news stories through browser **portal sites**. These offer headlines of breaking news, and links to the 'full story'.

✴ There are some online newspapers that only exist on the web. For example, see Indymedia (www.indymedia.org) and The Register (www. theregister.co.uk).

✴ Organisations that are in the news will publish press releases via their websites. For example, the government has sites in which news about new legislation is published, and the examination boards publish news of syllabus changes on their sites, as do publishers.

✴ Individuals – called bloggers – may also indulge in direct journalism through **blogging**. Blogs are online personal journals or diaries and tend to comment on topics of interest to the blogger. The best blogs are updated frequently, maybe daily or weekly, depending on the blogger.

PORTAL SITES
See page 100.

What does it mean?

BLOGGING
A blog is a private web page like a journal or diary which reveals personal information about the blogger.

YOUR TURN!

1 Visit http://uk.dir.yahoo.com/News_and_Media/Newspapers/Web_Directories/ and, from there, visit newspaper sites that are of interest to you.

2 Search for international news sites. Which ones are available in a language that you understand?

3 Visit http://www.headstar.com/egb/ and read the online publication: E-Government Bulletin.

4 Search for examples of blogs. How often are these sites updated? What topics are of interest to the blogger? Search for a blog that includes information of relevance to you.

5 Search for sites that provide news that is local to you, through your local council or Tourist Information Office.

6 Review your browser portal site. Does it provide the news coverage you require? What options does it offer, if any, for local news?

7 Using your History folder, create bookmarks to your favourite local, national and international newspapers, and any other sites you might want to return to.

REMEMBER
You know how to make a page your home page; see page 73.

Local news

All local councils (i.e. district, county, metropolitan and unitary) now have websites. The local councils use these sites to provide relevant information to local residents – such as dustbin collection arrangements over a bank holiday weekend and library opening hours – and to promote the local area.

In addition, some areas benefit from websites run by the local Tourist Information Office. For example, www.salcombeinformation.co.uk provides lots of information of relevance to tourists but is also useful for anyone moving into the Salcombe area permanently.

National and international news

National news is available on the Internet, not just for the UK but for almost all nations.

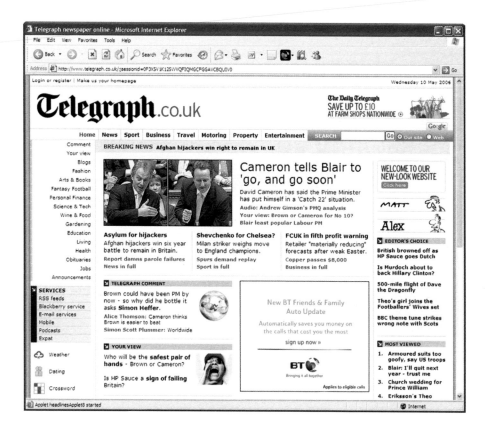

Because of language differences, these sites might be multi-lingual. Of the foreign ones that are published in the native tongue, some offer English translation options.

The choice of languages is often displayed as the flags of the various countries.

YOUR TURN!

1 Consider setting up a newspaper or browser portal site as your home page.

TV and radio

What does it mean?

HARD COPY
A copy produced on paper.

You can buy a **hard copy** magazine which gives you the TV and radio listings for one week. However, things change, and at short notice, so this information can become out of date and inaccurate. Instead, if you have access to the Internet, you can find the most up-to-date information on the WWW.

❋ Portal sites offer TV and radio listings as one of their features. You can arrange to have this information always on view on your 'front page'.

❋ Sites like the BBC's provide full listings of their TV and radio broadcast schedules.

To compete with the hardcopy magazines, many of these sites provide articles about those actors appearing onscreen. They can also provide useful links to other sites of interest.

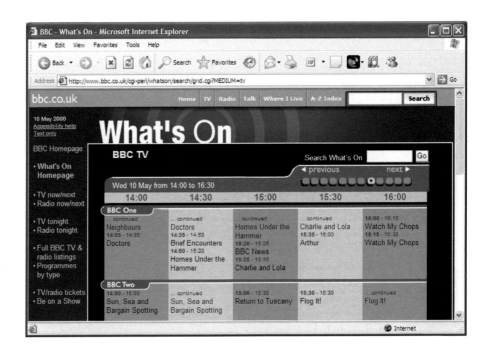

REMEMBER
You can listen to a radio programme after it has been broadcast; see page 105.

YOUR TURN!

1 Search for TV listings through your chosen portal site.
2 Visit the BBC site (you should have it bookmarked in your Favorite folder) and check what is on TV today.
3 Search for other sites that offer TV and radio schedule information. Bookmark any of these that you might want to visit again.

Corporate news

Many organisations have their own website, but may also have an **intranet** which is accessible only to employees of the organisation.

If your employer has an intranet, you will have received training as to how to gain access, and what information is available online for you.

One thing that does change every day, and which you can check on the Internet, are share prices.

The site www.ftse.com, for example, provides business news and up-to-date statistics.

YOUR TURN!

1 If your organisation has an intranet, explain to someone in your group who does not know, how it works and how you gain access. Do not divulge confidential information, such as your password.

2 Search the Internet for Stock Exchange news about three major companies that have been in the news in the last week.

Government

The WWW houses many government websites. Whatever your area of interest, there is almost certain to be a government website offering relevant information to you.

This section considers social services, business services, current initiatives, laws and legislation, central and local government issues of topical interest, and public statistics.

Directgov

The government has set up its own portal site, Directgov, which has links to sites operated by the individual government departments. Whatever information you require, www.direct.gov.uk aims to provide the links for you.

* Want to report graffiti?
* Want to renew your library books?
* Want to apply for a road tax disc online?
* Want to pay your council tax online?
* Need practical advice about how to complain?

Directgov offers **deep linking** to the correct local authority's website.

What does it mean?

DEEP LINKING
Instead of taking you to the home page of a website, deep linking takes you to a particular page within a site.

Business services

The government offers services to help small businesses and, through the www.sbs.gov.uk site, it provides the public, researchers, the media and policymakers with information about the Small Business Service and what it does.

A second site – called Business Link – is part of the Business Link national advice service. This site offers practical business information and provides links to a wide range of business support sites.

You can also search for local information based on your postcode. See www.businesslink.gov.uk.

Current initiatives

In the world of government, things change daily. To keep track, you might search on 'current initiatives'. If you do this on the sbs.gov.uk site, you should be rewarded with a lot of links to other sites. At the time of writing, such a search gave 159 Small Business Service pages and 47 pages from partner sites.

Laws and legislation

Legislation is passed – after a lengthy process – and the laws are enacted. The full text of any new Act is available online (www.opsi.gov.uk/acts.htm), but there are also sites which explain the legislation.

For example, if you search on OPSI, using the keywords 'data protection' and, in the Advanced criteria, stipulate 'Act', you will be given a link to the Data Protection Act. You could search, e.g. using *Google*, and this will lead you to the Information Commissioner's Office website (www.ico.gov.uk) as well as other sites, such as the Department for Constitutional Affairs (www.dca.gov.uk).

> **REMEMBER**
> You can use Advanced search tools to refine your search; see page 103.

YOUR TURN!

1 Explore the government portal site. Use it to access the NHSDirect site. Then go to the Self-help guide and use the body key. This is an example of an **image link**. Explore any conditions that are of interest to you or your family, and bookmark any pages that you might want to return to.

2 Visit the Small Business Service website and, from there, go to the Business Link site. Search for current initiatives.

3 Visit **www.theyworkforyou.com** and find out what has been happening in Parliament in the last week.

IMAGE LINK
See page 106.

What does it mean?

THEYWORKFORYOU. COM
This website aims to make it easy for people to keep tabs on their elected and unelected representatives in Parliament.

Central government

You have already seen a number of government sites, but there are others listed on a central website (www.number-10.gov.uk).

You can send an e-mail to the Prime Minister, watch a film of the government in action and subscribe for e-mail updates to be delivered direct to your desktop, or visit one of the sites set up for each government department.

* The Cabinet Office is at the centre of government and is responsible for coordinating policy and strategy across the other departments.

* The Department for Culture, Media and Sport aims to improve the quality of life for all, through cultural and sporting activities.

* The Department for Education and Skills is responsible for schools: nurseries through to higher education and including adult learners. Its stated purpose is to create opportunity, release potential and achieve excellence for all.

* The Department for Environment, Food & Rural Affairs aims to bring together the interests of farmers and the countryside, the environment and the rural economy. It tries to integrate environmental, social and economic objectives, and champion sustainable development as the way forward.

And there are many, many more listed.

There is also the website coordinated by HM Revenue & Customs (www.hmrc.gov.uk) where you can file your self-assessment tax form online and learn about tax credits and child benefits.

Local government

A website provides an ideal opportunity for a borough council to communicate with local residents.

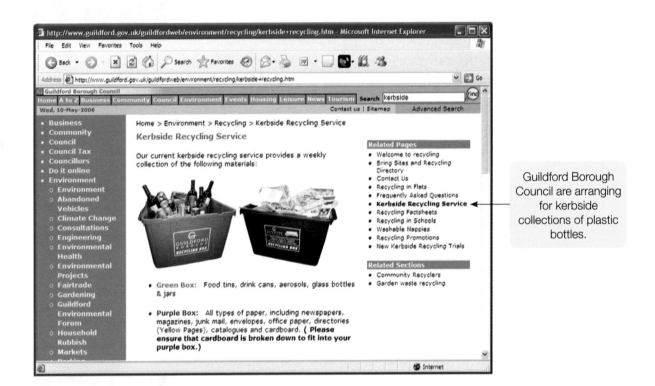

Guildford Borough Council are arranging for kerbside collections of plastic bottles.

REMEMBER
You can reach all government department sites by going to the portal site Directgov and searching on a key term.

YOUR TURN!

1 Visit the Cabinet Office website and read what has been done to prepare for emergencies (PFE).

2 Visit the site of the Department for Culture, Media and Sport. Look to see what information is available relating to the Olympic Games.

3 Visit the HM Revenue & Customs website and find out the deadline for filing a tax return.

4 Visit a local government services website and find out the arrangements for recycling waste in your area.

5 Refer to your History folder and bookmark any sites that you might want to revisit.

Public statistics

The Office for National Statistics (www.statistics.gov.uk) collects data on Britain's economy, population and society at national and local level, and publishes it. Some of this comes from the census data that is collected.

The data is used to help in decision-making about government policy but is also of interest to others who are planning for the future.

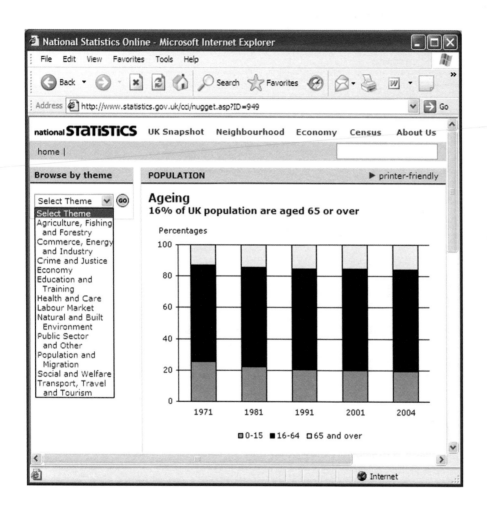

YOUR TURN!

1 Visit the National Statistics website and look for data on the demographics of the population of the UK. Confirm that we have an ageing population.

2 Find a graph that compares under 16s and over 65s, and save this image in your ECDL folder.

> **REMEMBER**
> You can copy an image from a web page and save it on your hard disk; see page 112.

European Parliament

The European Parliament is an elected single-chamber body. The Europarl site (www.europarl.eu.int) is multilingual and has content in all EU languages, with English as an option. The www.europarl.org.uk site is the UK office and is only presented in English.

A text only version of this page is available.

YOUR TURN!

1 Visit the European Parliament site at www.europarl.eu.int and opt for English.
   Click on the Parliament tab and select 'Parliament near you'. Click on the map to find out the contact details for the London and Edinburgh offices.
2 Visit the London office site at www.europarl.org.uk and find out the name of your MEP.
   Notice that you can view a 'Text only' version.

Consumer

This section focuses on your use of the Internet as a consumer: looking out for new offers, deciding what to buy, and then checking on prices and availability.

Instead of going out to the shops, you can shop online at one of the many online stores. You can also arrange to pay for the goods or services through your online banking account.

Online stores

The traditional corner shop saw its decline with the arrival of supermarkets. Now, in the Internet generation, some people have their groceries delivered to the door by the superstores.

Meanwhile, small specialist concerns can flourish on the Internet. Instead of the expensive overheads of premises, and a limited catchment of shoppers, the Internet provides specialist vendors with a global market.

Shopping

For many, the days of traipsing around the shops to find the best deal may well be over. Even if you want to buy at a store near you, you can check prices online before you venture out; this will save you time.

There are also websites that offer to check prices for you. These sites search the web for thousands of different products from hundreds of Internet stores and high street retailers and claim always to be on the lookout for bargains for you.

YOUR TURN!

1 Use a search engine and the keywords 'check prices' to locate some sites that offer a price checking service. Visit and bookmark two of those.

2 Imagine you need to buy an inkjet printer.
Use your bookmarked sites to locate the best buy.

3 Visit the online store recommended and check that an inkjet printer, at the price suggested, is available.

Banking online

The banks move with the times.

* **ATMs** were introduced to allow account holders to check balances and withdraw cash at times when the bank was closed. This also cut down queues inside the bank when it was open.

* Banks introduced telephone banking as an option to check your account balance. You are 'spoken to' by an automated voice which responds to whatever you key on your phone pad. Or you can wait to speak to a real person at a call centre, probably in Scotland or India. You are unlikely to have straightforward access to your local branch. It is also possible to pay bills by telephone.

* Nowadays, banks offer online banking, and you can do just about everything you would want to, from anywhere in the world, provided you have Internet access.

What does it mean?

ATM
Stands for automated teller machine.

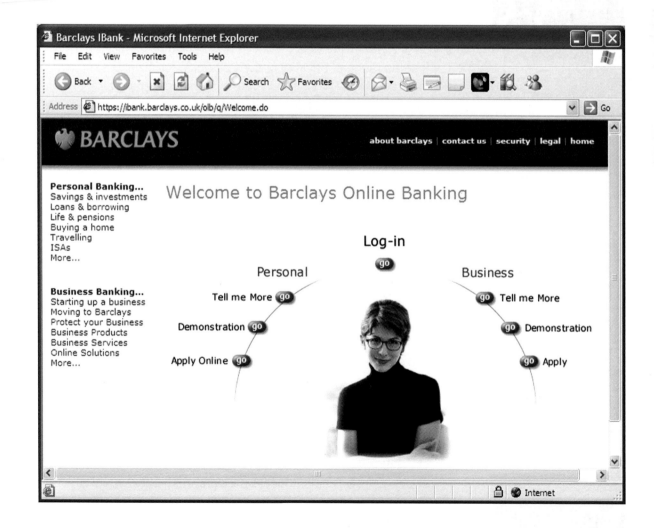

Banks are not the only financial institutions that offer an online service.

❊ If you own premium bonds, you will have a bond holder number. You can use this to access the National Savings & Investment site at www.nsandi.com and check whether you have won any prizes.

❊ If you open a savings account that pays interest, such as ING Direct (www.ingdirect.co.uk), you can check your statement online, and move money from savings into your personal current banking account and vice versa.

❊ If you have a credit card, the credit card company, such as Barclaycard or Egg, will provide options for viewing account details and certain transactions online.

Each of these accounts holds personal data about the account holder so there will be protection in the form of account numbers and one or more passwords, to try to prevent unauthorised access to the account.

> **REMEMBER**
> Choosing a password needs to be done with care; see page 123.

> **REMEMBER**
> When printing a web page, choose the printer-friendly version; see page 114.

YOUR TURN!

1 In Your Turn! on page 128, you were advised to consider online banking. If you have not yet registered, and plan to do so, do it now.

2 Look at the range of banking options available for moving money between accounts. What options are available for paying bills and setting up standing orders or direct debits?

3 Explore the options to print statements. Can you change the start and end dates? Is there a printer-friendly version?

Local entertainment

If you plan to go to the cinema, or to watch a play at your local theatre, you might look in your local free newspaper for details. You could also look on the Internet, as this option may allow you to book tickets and choose seats. For example, the Yvonne Arnaud Theatre in Guildford has a website at: www.yvonne-arnaud.co.uk.

❊ You can see what shows are planned.

❊ You can download a brochure in **PDF format**.

❊ There are instructions as to how to find the theatre, including all you need to know about travel and parking arrangements.

❊ You can join the mailing list, to receive e-mails about forthcoming shows.

The most useful feature is the option to book tickets and buy them online.

❊ If there are seats available, the reservation system offers you the number of seats you request in the area of the theatre that you choose from a diagram. It then gives you 15 minutes to make up your mind!

❊ Once you have found seats you like, you can proceed to pay for the seats using your credit card. The tickets may then be sent to you, or you might pick them up at the theatre just before the show.

What does it mean?

PDF
Stands for portable document format. To overcome layout problems, some documents are offered in PDF format. To read them you need Adobe Acrobat Reader, a freely available software package.

Cultural and sporting events

Organisers of cultural events at museums, art galleries and other venues provide information about forthcoming events on the web.

For example, www.londonforfun.com/events.htm gives details of the latest exhibitions, festivals and so on. After each brief description, there is a link to the website of the particular organisation responsible for the event. If you click on this link, a new window opens, and you then need to explore further to discover more about the event.

The WhatsOnWhen site (www.whatsonwhen.com) provides a global overview of events.

At the time of writing, this site was advertising an arts event celebrating the work of Matisse in Switzerland and a passionate religious festival in Spain that 'provides a glimpse into the soul of Spain'.

Sites that you visit are keen for you to return and, rather than rely on you to bookmark the site and return when it occurs to you, they invariably offer a free newsletter.

If you subscribe to this newsletter, by supplying your e-mail address, you will receive regular e-mailings full of new and exciting events, written in the hope that you might be tempted to return to the site.

The first time you receive the mailing, the spam filter might send it to your Bulk e-mail inbox, so you may need to flag it as 'not spam'.

> **REMEMBER**
> Spam is unsolicited mail, but bulk e-mails are assumed to be spam until you tell the spam filter otherwise; see page 80.

Travel

Travel is another area in which the Internet has transformed how transactions happen, especially for people booking holidays. How did it happen in the 'good old' days?

❊ You would go to a travel agent, and take home a pile of relevant brochures to pore over. You would then go back to the travel agent, and explain what you wanted.

❊ He or she would spend time on the telephone talking to hotels and airlines, trying to knit together a number of separate strands that would form your holiday.

❊ You would pay a deposit now, and the balance later.

❊ The paperwork would arrive through the post: flight tickets and other travel instructions.

Nowadays the process is much more streamlined.

❊ You can search for holiday offers on the web.

❊ You can book your own flights, accommodation, car hire and so on.

❊ You can pay for everything online, using a credit card.

So, if you wish, you can plan everything for yourself, and do the work that the travel agent would have done.

Recently, some airlines have introduced ticket-less flights. Having booked and paid for your travel on the Internet, you receive confirmation in an e-mail. You need to print this e-mail out – or at least write down a confirmation number – and you use this at the checking-in desk to prove you have bought a flight.

Travel agencies have had to move with the times. To retain a share of the holiday market, many now offer specialised holidays which require their skills, and they focus on good personal service to retain your custom.

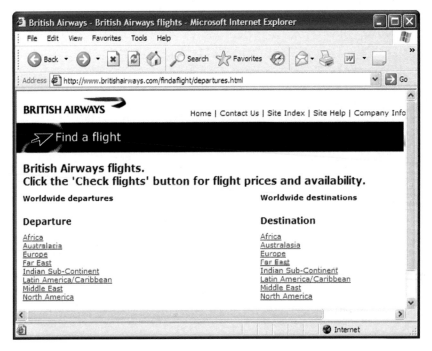

YOUR TURN!

1 Imagine that you wanted to visit some long lost relatives in Australia. Use the Internet to plan the travel arrangements for such a trip. Investigate airlines that provide flights between the UK and Australia. Can you stop somewhere en route? Or is it a direct flight?

2 A couple of friends from overseas are visiting you and have asked you to collect them from the airport. They are travelling with British Airways, flying in from Athens. Check the expected arrival times of flights from Athens.

3 You are planning a long weekend away for you and a friend. You would like to visit one of the European capitals. Your friend is vegetarian, and also needs a lot of leg room, so would prefer an aisle seat. Investigate the option for a cheap flight to France, Portugal, Spain, Italy or one of the islands in the Mediterranean. What options do you have regarding seat booking? Is there an option to specify special dietary needs?

Travelling by bus or train

Bus and coach operators plan their schedules ages in advance and these are printed for display at bus stops and railway stations. Printed booklets which focus on particular areas are small enough to keep in your wallet or handbag.

The operators also provide this information electronically and there are websites that rely on this information to help you to plan a journey without using your car.

For coach journeys, you could visit the National Express site (www.nationalexpress.com). If you prefer to 'let the train take the strain', the Trainline site (www.trainline.com) can be used to find out times, book tickets and reserve seats for any train operator in mainland UK. Alternatively, if you know which train service you need, you could go direct to their site, e.g. Virgin Trains (www.virgintrainsfares.co.uk).

Other sites, such as Xephos (www.internet. xephos.com) offer a subscription service. You must register to access the information available, providing only your name and e-mail address. After a free trial period (at the time of writing, 7 days or 100 hits), you will be invited to either take out a monthly subscription (£2 pcm) or a pay as you go (£5 for 250 hits) to continue to access the site.

YOUR TURN!

1 You belong to a club, and it has been decided to organise a coach trip to a place in the UK of interest to your club members.
(This could be a trip to a sports event, such as the tennis tournament at Wimbledon, or an exhibition such as one at the Birmingham NEC centre, or a show in London or Edinburgh – whatever interests you.)
Investigate the timing and price of using a scheduled coach service – rather than hiring a coach, or going by car or train.

2 In the Your Turn! on page 147, you planned a trip to Australia.
Use the Internet to find out what coach/train options you have to travel from your home to the departure airport, so that you arrive in good time for check-in.

3 Some friends who do not have Internet access have accepted an invitation to visit you. They live 200–250 miles from you (choose a suitable location for their home!).
Search the Internet for details as to how they might travel to you by coach or train.
Use Multimap (or a similar website) to check the route they might take if they were to travel by car.
Use the Multimap site also to suggest a route so you can see exactly how many miles they would need to drive.

4 In the Your Turn! on page 147, you planned a trip to a European capital. Review your plans, and check whether there is a coach alternative which might suit you (and your pocket) better.

> **REMEMBER**
> You have visited the Multimap site before; see page 114.

Accommodation

Finding somewhere to stay is often an integral part of the planning of a holiday.

Many hotels – all of the large chains and many of the individually run hotels – have websites.

The sites often include photos of the bedrooms, maybe the lounge area or restaurant, and the grounds.

There may be additional information, such as a map, to help you to locate the hotel on arrival, and details of local facilities (beach, amusements and so on).

Searching for a hotel is straightforward.

* If you want to stay in a particular hotel, or chain of hotels, a search on the name should return the relevant website link.

* If you don't know the name of a hotel, but want to stay in a particular town, searching on 'hotel Salcombe', for example, will give you a hit list of several hotels in the Salcombe area.

Checking availability and booking online is also available for those hotels who have developed their website sufficiently to incorporate this functionality. Otherwise, the site should provide enough contact information to enable you to telephone and make a reservation.

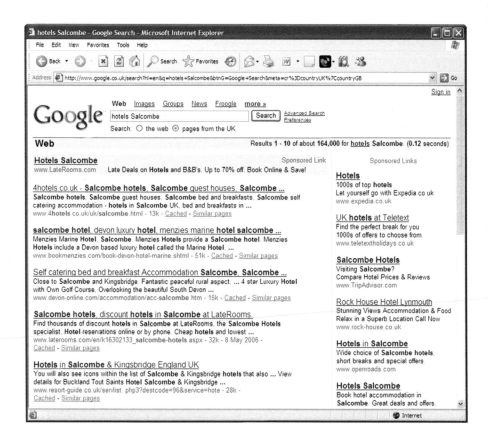

Checking availability online usually involves completing a form with certain information:

✴ date of arrival

✴ number of persons/type of accommodation required

✴ number of nights.

The website is linked to a database, which is kept up to date as bookings are taken. So, there should be no chance of arriving at the hotel to discover a double-booking error.

YOUR TURN!

1 In the travel plans for your trip to Australia (Your Turn! Activity 1 on page 147, and Your Turn! Activity 2 on page 148), you could stop over en route in Singapore or Hong Kong. Investigate these options to find out the costs and time implications.

2 In the travel plans for a long weekend in a European capital (Your Turn! Activity 3 on page 147), you should have decided by now on one or more possible destinations, and know the costs of these flights.
Check hotel room availability and price for your first and second choice of capital. Compare the total cost of each holiday destination.

3 The friends who plan to visit you (Your Turn! Activity 3 on page 148) have asked for a recommendation for a local B&B. They may need to bring their dog with them, so will need dog-friendly accommodation. Search the Internet to find at least three options for them.

Education/Training

You may have already visited the website of the Department for Education and Skills (www.dfes.gov.uk). As well as statements about educational issues (such as bullying, testing and qualifications), it provides links to finding the right educational resource at all levels:

* finding the right nursery or childcare
* finding the right primary or secondary school, or academy or specialist school
* finding the right college or university course, full- or part-time
* finding work, training, career information and voluntary work opportunities.

DIRECTGOV
See page 136.

It offers search options to help you to locate the educational establishment that will suit you. Some of these links take you to a one-stop source of information about public services: **Directgov** (www.direct.gov.uk).

From Directgov, you can then locate schools, colleges and universities – most of whom boast a website; and each one listing the courses and training available.

Evening classes

Adult education is available during the day but, for people who go to work during the day, the main opportunity for learning lies in the evening classes that are run in schools and colleges outside normal teaching hours.

Evening classes might introduce a practical skill like painting and drawing, bricklaying, gardening or cookery. Or you might want to learn a new language, or learn how to teach one. Or, you might want to concentrate on the more traditional subjects that lead to examinations and qualifications.

YOUR TURN!

1 Use the Internet to search for venues near you where adult education classes are being held. Make a note of the term dates.

2 Imagine that your neighbour does not have Internet access, but plans to buy a computer and would like to enrol on a beginners' class. Search the Internet to see what courses are available at a centre near you.

3 In preparation for your European weekend away (Your Turn! Activity 2 on page 149), you decide you would like to attend a beginners' class in a foreign language spoken in the country you will be visiting. Find out what courses are available, and whether you can book online.

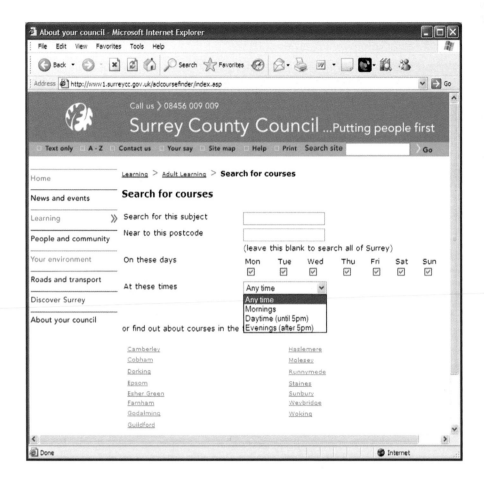

E-learning opportunities

What does it mean?

E-LEARNING
Means using materials
that are published on the
WWW for self-study.

The government's long-term vision for e-learning – in the next five years and the next ten years – is explained by the DfES on their website: www.dfes.gov.uk/publications/e-strategy/.

If, for personal reasons, you cannot commit to attend a course the same day each week for several weeks, you can still study – by using the Internet for e-learning. Depending on your area of interest, there are lots of subjects you can study through e-learning.

❊ If you are interested in local history, there may be some learning resources which will reveal information about where you live. For example, the Discover Isle of Wight history site (http://history.iwight.com) has a number of learning resources which encourage families to take an active interest in local and family history.

❊ If you want to learn a language, the BBC offers self-contained online courses for several different languages – enough to get by on a holiday. It also offers games and quizzes to make learning fun.

❊ The BBC – through its BBCi Get Writing site – offers courses for those interested in creative writing. It also offers a search facility if you are looking for a group local to you for a small range of courses: journalism, literacy, writing and English Language.

Some e-learning courses are free; others are available for a small fee. See, for example, www.learners.org.uk.

A good starting point to find out more about e-learning opportunities is the e-Learning Centre (www.e-learningcentre.co.uk), which has a showcase of good e-learning projects.

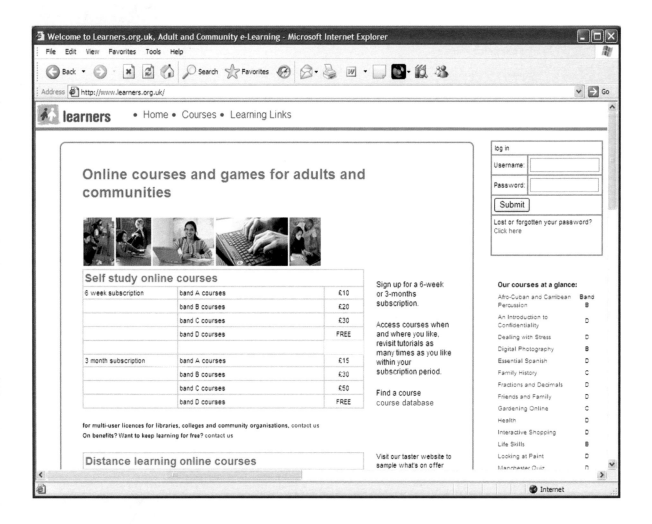

YOUR TURN!

1 Use the Internet to locate e-learning opportunities for someone who wants to learn Spanish. Bookmark any sites that provide games or fun activities for the learner. Group these bookmarks in a folder called Spanish.

2 Visit the www.learners.org.uk site and look at some of the free courses available.

3 Visit www.languagesonline.org.uk. To play the games on this site, you need Adobe **Flash Player**.
If your computer does not already have Flash Player, follow the instructions to download this free software.

What does it mean?

FLASH PLAYER
Software needed for some animations to work onscreen.

Library sites

Long before Internet use became so common, libraries were the main point of reference for most researchers.

Now, on the Internet, much the same information is available, without your having to leave the house.

If you search *Google* for 'library sites' in the UK, the first hit is for Leeds University, which boasts many fine libraries on the campus (www.leeds.ac.uk/library/sites/).

The John Rylands University Library has made a study of library websites (http://rylibweb.man.ac.uk/pubs/libraries.html), and recommends the Sheffield University site (www.shef.ac.uk/library/) for well laid out pages and for keeping images simple but effective, and thus reducing download time. They also recommend South Ayrshire Public Library (www.south-ayrshire.gov.uk/libraries/) for its links to online newspapers and magazines, and to its Kids website. Many other sites are recommended too.

Each of these sites provide specialist search tools to help you to find what you are looking for.

> **REMEMBER**
> You can access the website for your local library through the Directgov portal site.

Library sites - Leeds University Library - Microsoft Internet Explorer

File   Edit   View   Favorites   Tools   Help

Back   ·   Search   Favorites

Address http://www.leeds.ac.uk/library/sites/   Go

Welcome to
LEEDS UNIVERSITY LIBRARY

University of Leeds Home | Campusweb | Text only display   Search Library website: Search

MENU   INDEX   You are here: Library > Library sites   Was this page useful?   yes   no

I want to . . .
Go to Library Home
Search the Catalogue
Check my Library record
See resources for my subject
Use electronic resources

How do I . . .
Use the Library
Find items in the Library
Check the opening hours
Contact the Library
Borrow and renew books

Leeds University Library Sites

On this page:
▼ Brotherton Library
▼ Edward Boyle Library
▼ Health Sciences Library
▼ Bretton Hall Campus
▼ St James's
▼ University Archive
▼ University Gallery
▼ Wakefield Campus
▼ Campus Library Locations

Done   Internet

Having online access to your local library means that you can check what books you have on loan and when they are due back, and you can reserve books, and so on. Of course, you still need to go to the library to collect and return books but, with the introduction of **e-books**, this too may become a thing of the past.

Some libraries organise reading groups: some of these groups meet face to face; others can discuss the books using online messaging.

Bookwire, a site (www.bookwire.com) owned by the publishers Bowker, features the authors published by them, their bestsellers, e-books, as well as a directory guiding you to even more book resources on the Internet.

If you like crime and mystery books, you could visit the Mystery Reader site (www.themysteryreader.com) to read reviews and learn more about the authors of such books.

YOUR TURN!

1 Use the Internet to access the website for your local library. Check at what times the library is open.

2 If you have a library card, access your account by entering your library card number and your **PIN**. Check that the details of your address and your contact details are correct. Amend them if they are wrong.

3 Look to see what events are being held at the library during the next month. If the library pages are part of a larger website for the county council, you will see details of events for the whole county.

4 Check whether the library has computers on which you could access the Internet. Check whether you can book time on one of these computers.

Employment

Prior to the Internet, jobs were advertised in newspapers or filled through private recruitment agencies. There were – and still are – these options, plus the government-run Jobcentres, which aim to find work for the unemployed.

Prospective employers write a job specification or person specification, and prospective employees write a CV.

The trick is then to match the two!

Job vacancy sites

If you search on *Google* using the keywords 'seek a job', the hit list offers more than 100 million sites.

✳ Some sites are government run. The Jobseeker site (www.jobcentreplus.gov.uk) explains the benefits available to those who are out of work. It also links to pages which help you to search for a job.

✳ Some sites are run by universities and offer advice to graduates (e.g. http://careers.lancs.ac.uk/newcareers/graduate/work.htm).

✳ Some are recruitment agencies who will try to place you in work, and will earn a commission from the employer for doing so.

✳ Some agencies are geared for a particular type of person. For example, Blue Arrow through their **OPEN** site (www.bluearrow.co.uk/open/) try to place athletes within companies who will support their training regime.

✳ Some are organisations who have vacancies and want to recruit staff without going through a recruitment agency and paying their fees.

! HANDY TIP

If a deep link (one that points to a particular page) fails to load a page, go to the home page instead. Then, use the search facilities to find what you want.

What does it mean?

OPEN
Stands for Olympic and Paralympic Employment Network.

YOUR TURN!

In this activity, the focus is on 'plumber' vacancies.
If you wish, replace the keyword 'plumber' with one which is more relevant for you.

1 Using a search engine, browse for job advertisements. Start by using keywords that describe the type of job and the location, e.g. 'plumber' and 'Surrey'. Follow some of the links.

2 Go to the government Jobseeker site and see what jobs for plumbers in Surrey can be found through this route.

3 Search instead for 'plumbing firms' and then look for companies who are advertising jobs for plumbers.

Applying for a job online

Having found a job that you would like to apply for, the next step is to complete an application form.

For some vacancies, this can be done online. Doing so online immediately signals to the prospective employer that you are computer literate.

The web page http://jobsearch.about.com/od/jobapplications/a/jobapplication_3.htm provides guidance as to how best to complete an online form.

It offers a sample application form that you can download and complete. This will require you to collect information that most prospective employers will ask for, and give you some practice in completing an application form.

It also offers advice on how to write your CV and a letter of application.

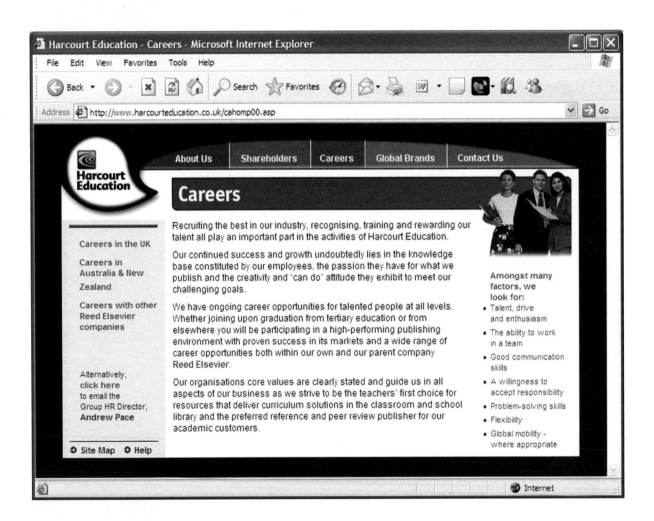

HOW TO... Complete a job application online

 1 Take your time. Do not be tempted to complete and submit an online form immediately. You should take the same amount of time and care as you would with a paper application form.

 2 Print off the form and work on a hard copy first. Or copy and paste it into a word processing package.

 3 Because online forms are full of formatting, paste them into *Notepad* first. Or if you have a Paste Special option in your word processing software, use this and select Plain text.

 4 There may be optional and compulsory fields. Be sure to complete the compulsory fields. And aim to complete optional sections too. If they ask for more detailed background information, it is your opportunity to impress the employer as to what is special about you.

 5 If you are working on a word processor, do not rely on the spell checker. Do a thorough proof check too.

 6 Print the online form and read it carefully, several times, before submitting it.

 7 Save a copy of the completed form for yourself. Use the browser's File/Save As option. For a filename, use the company name and the date. Save it in a separate folder and name the folder, e.g. Job applications.

YOUR TURN!

1 Visit http://jobsearch.about.com/od/jobapplications/a/jobapplication_3.htm and read what is said about completing job application forms.

2 Browse the sites of companies that you and others in your group work for. How are jobs advertised? Is there an option to apply online?

3 Complete an online application form.

Company pensions

The average life expectancy in the UK is increasing. You could check this by visiting the Office for National Statistics (page 139)! As we live longer, we may work a bit longer, but can expect to spend many years as retired pensioners. So, the amount of money we might expect is important.

Information on pensions is available on the WWW.

❋ The BBC News section may have an article giving up-to-date information on the state of the pension market. An article written in February 2002 gives a basic guide to pensions and was still available at the time of writing (March 2006): http://news.bbc.co.uk/1/hi/business/1829193.stm.

❋ The pension companies, such as Standard Life and Scottish Widows, provide both advice and information about their own products.

❋ The Directgov site explains how you might want to contribute to both a company and personal pension plan.

❋ Sites like iVillage explain the main types of company pension, while others, like i-resign, explain what can happen if you want to change jobs.

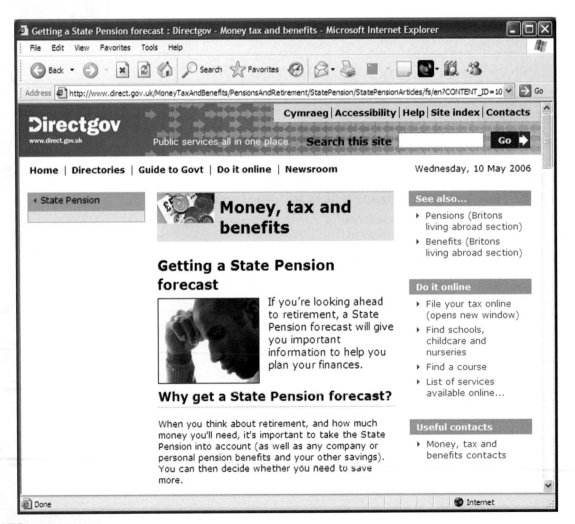

1 Visit each of the sites mentioned on page 158. Bookmark any that you might want to visit again.

2 If you already have a pension, visit the website of your pension company. If they offer a registration option, sign on so that you can receive mailings automatically.

3 If you don't have any pension arrangements in place, read about your options and consider whether you might be advised to take one out. Search for information on pensions so that you can make an informed choice about which type of pension you might need and which pension company to approach.

Health

Alexander Pope, in *An Essay on Criticism*, said: 'A little knowledge is a dangerous thing' and then went on to qualify this: 'Drink deep, or taste not the Pierian spring: there shallow draughts intoxicate the brain, and drinking largely sobers us again.'

Health is one area where this saying is perhaps true. Having access to so much health information on the Internet is not always helpful though. If you didn't think you were ill before you access the information, by the time you have checked out the symptoms, you may think you are!

Healthcare Commission

The Healthcare Commission promotes improvement in the quality of both the NHS and the independent healthcare sector (www. healthcarecommission.org.uk). One of its duties is to assess the performance of healthcare organisations. So, any complaints about healthcare, if not resolved locally, fall into its lap.

The Healthcare Commission produces a monthly newsletter which includes articles on issues such as reducing obesity in children, and conducts surveys, e.g. on patients with strokes. The current newsletter is available online – and back copies can be downloaded as PDF files.

> **REMEMBER**
> The government portal site Directgov has links to relevant sites, such as NHSDirect, for health issues.

> **REMEMBER**
> PDF files can be read using Adobe Acrobat Reader, a free software package.

YOUR TURN!

1 Search on 'healthcare' and see what sites appear in the hit list. Visit any that interest you, and bookmark any that you might want to visit again.

2 Visit the Healthcare Commission site. Search for information on your local health services, and find out the performance rating of your nearest hospital trust.

Alternative medicines

The WWW is an excellent source of information about alternative medicines. There are many sites offering alternative medicines for sale, and advice as to which ones will cure which disease. However, you should exercise caution. Is a site just trying to sell you a product?

NCCAM (National Centre for Complementary and Alternative Medicine) makes available the Combined Health Information Database (http://nccam.nih.gov/), which contains information on alternative medicine research not available in other government databases. The NCCAM site invites you to be an informed consumer. It also offers lots of information on popular health topics like acupuncture, arthritis and cancer.

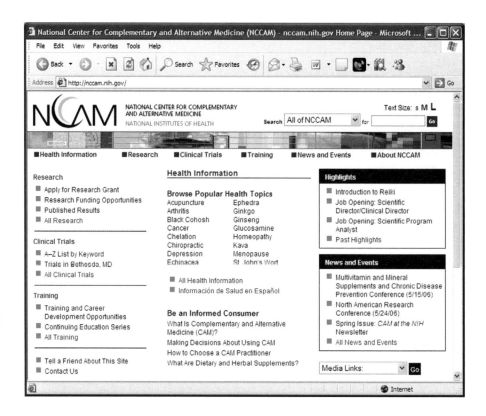

YOUR TURN!

1 Visit the NCCAM site and search for information of interest to you.
2 Search for sites that sell herbal medicines.
   How sure are you as to the quality of the products?
   How sure are you that the advice you are given is sound?
3 Search for information on alternative medicine from a site you think you can trust – like the BBC site (http://news.bbc.co.uk/1/hi/health/425986.stm).

Private healthcare

Although the NHS offers healthcare and, especially, emergency healthcare, more and more people are turning to private health care – those that can afford to, that is.

Organisations such as BUPA (www.bupa.co.uk) offer a range of health cover insurance policies, so that you pay a monthly premium and then expect to have your medical bills paid if and when you fall ill. They also offer health care information and advice.

Nuffield Hospitals (www.nuffieldhospitals.org.uk), the longest standing group of independent hospitals and a not-for-profit organisation, offers healthcare that is affordable to as many people as possible. It treats the private, medically insured, self-payers and NHS patients – and offers treatments such as hip replacements and laser eye surgery.

YOUR TURN!

1 If you already have medical insurance, visit the site of your insurer. Bookmark any pages of special interest.
2 If you do not have cover, search the WWW for information about private medical care.
   What might it cost? What might you expect to be treated for, free of further charge?

Interest groups

Whatever your interest, there is almost certainly a website that caters for you.

This section considers how groups – such as community groups, voluntary groups, and online discussion groups – use the Internet to share information and ideas.

Community groups

The WWW is full of advice about community groups.
* If you visit www.community.gov.au you will learn about communities in Australia.
* The UK site www.urbanforum.org.uk offers advice as to how you might get involved with voluntary and community groups.
* Directgov offers advice as to how to apply for funding for a community group (www.direct.gov.uk/HomeAndCommunity).

Some sites offer services to community groups.
* Tate Modern (www.tate.org.uk) offers introductory gallery talks for community groups. These are free of charge, take place mainly in the galleries and can be tailor-made to suit all interests or abilities.

> **REMEMBER**
> The last bit of a URL can tell you the location of a site. 'au' stands for Australia.

✽ Learning at Somerset House (www.courtauld.ac.uk) collaborates with a wide range of community groups, including clients of mental health services, adults with physical and learning disabilities, elders organisations, centres for asylum seekers and refugees and housing associations. Gallery talks, which can be followed up by practical art workshops, are provided free of charge. These sessions are tailor-made in order to suit the interests and needs of every group.

Voluntary groups

The WWW provides a useful way for voluntary groups to advertise what they do and to attract new volunteers.

Because volunteers usually have to appear in person – e.g. to work in a charity shop, or drive patients to and from hospital, or visit people who have been affected by a crime – many of the sites focus on a particular location or area.

✽ CamNet (www.cam.net.uk) lists charities and other voluntary and specialist interest groups operating in the Cambridge area.

✽ locallife (www.locallife.co.uk) provides links to organisations according to the area you select.

If you want to volunteer for work abroad, then the VSO site (www.vso.org.uk) provides all the information you need.

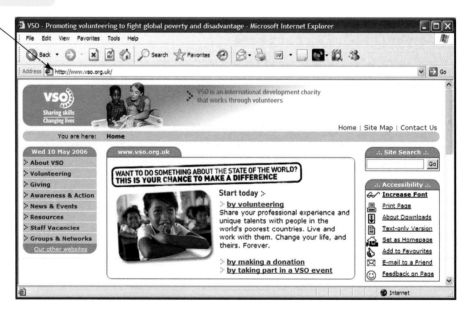

YOUR TURN!

1 Use the Internet to locate a community group local to your home or place of work.

2 Search for information on a voluntary group attached to a school or hospital close to your home.

Online discussion groups

Online discussion groups exist to provide a meeting point for people who share a common interest and/or want to meet other people in the virtual world of the Internet.

Discussion group systems are sometimes called message boards, bulletin boards or forums. (They are not the same as live chat systems.)

The organisation that sets up the discussion group opens up a form of communication which allows the members of the group to initiate new **threads** on which particular issues might be discussed, and to post comments on these threads.

This communication can be difficult to control, so it needs to be moderated. Moderation involves humans 'watching' every posting on a thread and intervening if the comments contravene whatever rules have been laid down.

Rules, such as the ones listed here, should be stated in clear terms and made available to all members.

* No insulting, threatening or provoking language.
* No inciting hatred on the basis of race, religion, gender, nationality, sexuality or other personal characteristics.
* No swearing, using hate-speech or making obscene or vulgar comments.
* No illegal behaviour such as committing libel, condoning illegal activity, contempt of court, or breach of copyright.
* No **spamming**.
* No impersonating another member, or using multiple identities.
* No posting of off-topic comments.

Discussion groups may be open or closed.

* An open group allows anyone with access to the site to join in.
* A closed group is restricted, so access is usually password controlled. The membership of the group can be by invitation; or prospective members might apply and be invited to join if they meet certain criteria.

What does it mean?

THREAD
A string of comments (or tiles) forming a conversation between the members of a group.

What does it mean?

SPAMMING
Adding the same comment repeatedly or across different groups.

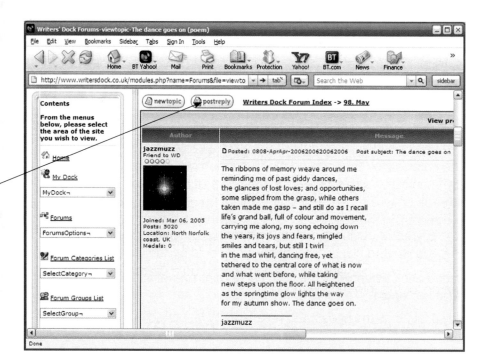

To write a review of jazzmuzz's poem, click on the postreply button. Your comment will appear further down the thread.

YOUR TURN!

1 Writers' Dock (www.writersdock.co.uk) is a website community for amateur and professional writers of poetry, short stories, non-fiction, and so on. The membership is free and members sign on using a pseudonym. Work is then posted and reviews are given. There are also discussion threads on topics that interest members.

Visit the Writers' Dock website and look around. Join up and post a message.

2 Look for other sites with discussion groups on a topic of particular interest to you. Start a new thread and join in the discussion on one or two other threads.

Business

Most businesses now have a website. If you apply for a job within an organisation and are invited for interview, instead of having to research the organisation by trying to get hold of a company brochure or looking them up in trade journals, you can do all your research on the Internet.

Sources of business information

If you know the name of the company you are researching, using that as a search key is most likely to provide a link to the appropriate site.

If you are not sure of the name of the organisation, or are looking for one to meet your needs, there are sites that will help you to track down an organisation's website.

* The UK Small Business Directory offers a service to businesses to advertise their websites free of charge. It states that 13,000 businesses are registered.

* TheLocalWeb (www.thelocalweb.net) claims to have a directory of 640,000 business websites. You can search on product/service or by company name, or use the classification system which then leads to a finer search. You can enter a postcode, too, so that you can locate businesses near you.

* RBA (Rhodes-Blakeman Associates) provides links to business sites on the Internet through its website (www.rba.co.uk). This organisation evaluates company information, such as share price.

Some types of business are required to register with Companies House, so if you want to check a company, you could go the Companies House website (www.companieshouse.gov.uk) and do a search. There is a charge for this information though.

Internet, intranet, extranet ...

According to Answers.com:

* An **intranet** is a privately maintained computer network accessed only by authorised persons, usually the members or employees of the organisation that owns it.

* An **extranet** is an extension of an intranet, especially over the WWW, enabling communication between those within the organisation and those outside it, and with the option of those outside having limited access to its intranet.

> **! HANDY TIP**
> If you are not sure what a word means, search on 'Definition' and the word.

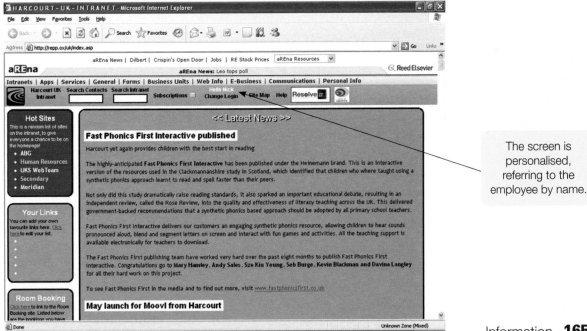

The screen is personalised, referring to the employee by name.

YOUR TURN!

1 Explore the websites mentioned on pages 164-5, and use them to locate organisations in your local neighbourhood. What information is available about these organisations?

2 If available, access your company intranet or extranet. Share information about accessing information via intranets and extranets with others in your group.

Record of achievement

Tick the boxes as you work through this course. When you have ticked everything you should be ready to take the examination.

BLOCK 2: Information search

	Done	Revised
SEARCHING		
What is a search engine?	☐	☐
Keyword searches	☐	☐
Combining criteria	☐	☐
Searching by navigating	☐	☐
Searching and browsing	☐	☐
Using Copy in a browser window	☐	☐
Saving an image from a web page	☐	☐
Saving a web page	☐	☐
Printing a web page	☐	☐
Bookmarking a favourite web page	☐	☐
PRECAUTIONS		
Internet exposure to risks	☐	☐
Viruses	☐	☐
Anti-virus software	☐	☐
Securing personal data	☐	☐
Consumer rights	☐	☐
Website integrity	☐	☐
Parental controls	☐	☐
INFORMATION		
News	☐	☐
Government	☐	☐
Consumer	☐	☐
Travel	☐	☐
Education/Training	☐	☐
Employment	☐	☐
Health	☐	☐
Interest groups	☐	☐
Business		

Block 3

e-Participation

In this block, you are introduced into the exciting world of online resources and services.

✳ Focusing on the same nine areas as Block 2, you will have the opportunity to build your confidence in carrying out everyday tasks such as buying a CD or a book, paying a bill, banking online or making a holiday reservation.

✳ You will access a variety of information services and learn how to carry out tasks such as looking up details, form filling and submitting information, so that you could, for example, enrol on a course, or book a doctor's appointment, or take part in an online discussion forum.

✳ You will revisit the issues and risks associated with using the Internet, concentrating on security threats in credit card transactions, and the importance of checking data in online forms.

✳ You will also learn to take precautionary measures when using the Internet for e-participation.

Lifeskills and benefits from use

When you have completed Block 3, you will have completed your studies for the e-Citizen course.

This block of work will give you:

* an appreciation of the Internet services available
* confidence to use the Internet services securely
* the skills to interact online so that you can benefit from commercial and
* government services that are offered on the Internet
* the skills to use government services and meet the e-Citizen's statutory obligations.

You should then be ready to tackle the Block 3 questions in the test. Be sure to revise all three blocks before taking the test.

Online services

In this section, you will learn skills that will give you the confidence to carry out everyday tasks such as buying a CD or a book online, paying a bill, banking online or making a holiday reservation. You will carry out a number of tasks, such as filling in a tax return, submitting a job application, enrolling on a course, making a doctor's appointment or taking part in an online discussion forum.

What is an online form?

Forms that you encounter on the WWW are similar to those you complete on paper. They are also similar to data entry forms used in spreadsheet and database applications.

Some of the data you enter on the WWW will most likely end up in a database. The web form you complete is a data entry form for the database, or something very similar.

During this course, you have already completed web forms, or elements of a form, perhaps without realising it.

✳ When you want to visit a site, you enter the URL in the address bar of your browser before pressing Go.

✳ When composing a new e-mail, you enter the data for the To, Subject and Message fields before pressing Send.

✳ When you use a search engine, you enter the keywords before pressing Search. If you do an advanced search, you make selections to narrow down your search – and indicate this by checking boxes, and picking things from a list.

PERSONAL DATA
See page 122.

Onscreen quotations

On some sites, before the site host can help you, you have to supply some **personal data**.

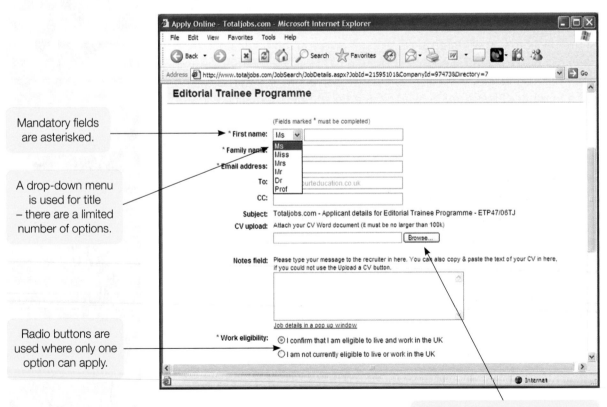

Mandatory fields are asterisked.

A drop-down menu is used for title – there are a limited number of options.

Radio buttons are used where only one option can apply.

Rather than having to remember the filename and folder for your CV, you can browse to locate it.

For example, if you are thinking about buying a new computer, you might visit the Dell website and choose the various parts of the computer: the amount of memory, and the peripherals such as a printer or scanner. Having made your choice, you might proceed to buy the computer.

Wherever you need to enter such data, you will be presented with a form that is designed to help you to enter your personal details accurately and efficiently.

This section now looks at the most common ways you might be asked to enter data into a web form.

✳ It looks at the components of a form, such as fields, menus, check boxes and buttons, so that you understand how to complete a form properly.

✳ It looks at how the system makes sure the data you enter is accurate, and the error messages you might see if you do anything 'wrong'; see page 177.

✳ It considers (on page 180) the security aspects of divulging data on the Internet, and how you might protect yourself from **identity fraud**.

What does it mean?

IDENTITY FRAUD
Using someone else's personal data, such as credit card number, to obtain goods or monies fraudulently is a criminal offence.

YOUR TURN!

1 Visit the Dell site and look at the forms you might need to complete if you were to want to buy a new computer.

2 Search the WWW for an insurance company and look at the form you would need to complete to get a quote for your car insurance.

How online forms work

A form is designed to collect data. The form asks a number of questions and you have to answer them. Questions can be open or closed.

✳ An **open question** gives you free rein to respond however you like, e.g. 'What is your occupation?'

✳ For **closed questions**, the form can offer options from which you choose one, e.g. a question may expect a YES/NO answer, or one from a few choices.

There are some answers which depend on what you have entered so far; and, for each type of answer, there is a form field type which is just right to collect your data.

Fields

Every item of data that you enter on a form goes into a **field**. Some of the fields are optional; some of them are **mandatory**.

Your form will not be accepted until you satisfactorily complete all the mandatory fields.

YOUR TURN!

1 Open your e-mail software. Start to compose a new e-mail. Look at the spaces on the e-mail form for places where you can type something. These are the fields. Which fields are optional? Which fields are mandatory? To test it out, omit one or more fields and try sending the e-mail. Under what circumstances will the e-mail not be sent?

2 Using a search engine such as *Google*, select Advanced search. Look at how you are asked to specify your criteria. Which fields are optional? Which are mandatory?

Tabbing

⚠ WARNING! If you are entering text into a field, such as the message field in an e-mail, tabbing acts like it normally does; it jumps to the next tab stop.

Part of the design process for a form is deciding the order in which you might best enter the data. The forms are laid out to match this order. Sometimes this means working from top to bottom, and sometimes it involves working from left to right. To work in any other direction would be nonsensical.

When you complete one field, the cursor may jump to the 'next' field. It may know which one is next because the designer has set up the **tab order**. (Note, though, that not all forms are so well designed!)

If, when you complete entering the data for a text field, you press Tab instead of Enter, the cursor should jump to the next logical field for you to fill in. If this is an optional field and you want to skip it, just press Tab again. This is called tabbing through the form and, because you do not have to use the mouse, it could speed up data entry.

YOUR TURN!

1 Open your e-mail software. Start to compose a new e-mail. Starting in the To field, tab through the form without entering any data.

2 Using a search engine such a *Google*, select Advanced search. Tab through this form to see the route that you are expected to take.

3 Go to a site that offers car insurance. Browse until you reach a form which asks for your personal details. Tab through the form, entering no data at all, but thinking about which details you think the insurance company are entitled to ask for. Press the button to submit your form. What happens? Which fields are mandatory?

Pop-up and pull-down menus

Text fields such as the one for the URL in a browser address bar, or the keywords in a search engine, allow you to enter whatever you like. Sometimes, the question is closed and the answer to it has to be limited. Also, since the reason for asking a question is to analyse your response in some way, data is often categorised.

❊ Personal details such as gender (male, female), age range (under 18, 19–30, 31–45 …) can be categorised into clear groups. You belong to only one such group.

❊ Personal details such as location (country, county or town) and nationality must match recognised answers, and these can be presented as an alphabetical list. For lists of countries, some cite Great Britain while others put United Kingdom (or UK); the difference between these two is sometimes missed.
Sometimes, the most common answers appear at the top of the list. Sometimes, a category called 'Other' is used to group together the less important answers.

❊ For a motor insurance quotation, the model and make of car must be one of a limited number available. This list changes with each new model that is introduced, so the database 'behind' the form has to be kept up to date.

❊ To buy a product online, you first choose a product list. If you want to buy the product, it has to be in stock, so the form must be linked to the vendor's database, tracking the availability of each product line.

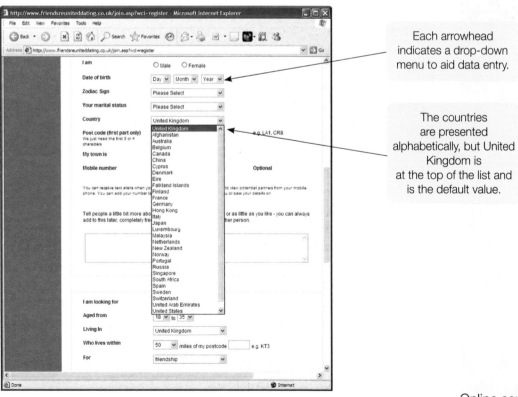

Each arrowhead indicates a drop-down menu to aid data entry.

The countries are presented alphabetically, but United Kingdom is at the top of the list and is the default value.

One way of limiting the data options is the pop-up or pull-down menu. Other methods (radio buttons and check boxes) are considered on page 177.

Rather than ask you to type in a lot of text information, a pop-up or pull-down menu provides a less error-prone way for you to communicate your data.

The availability of a menu tends to be shown by a triangular arrowhead. When the list is on view, if it is longer than the available window size, you can use the **scroll bar** to scan through all the items. To select an item, click on it (or use the arrow keys and press Enter).

YOUR TURN!

1 Return to the online form for car insurance. Notice which fields allow you to enter free text.

2 Tab through the form looking for fields which provide a menu. Click on one of these. Use the scroll bar, if necessary, to see all the options.

Screen buttons

To support you while completing a form, screen buttons may appear on or around a form.

✳ A screen button may offer help or additional information. For example, you should have read the terms and conditions associated with a purchase before proceeding to pay, and there may be a box you have to tick to say you have read them. Clicking a screen button will open a new window and display the terms and conditions, so that you can read them.

✳ Screen buttons may also be used to provide an option, such as to print a copy of the form.

Screen buttons, when pressed, take you away from completing the form.

✳ If it results in a new window being opened, closing the window that opens will take you back to the form.

✳ If a new window does not open, pressing the browser's Back button may also take you back to the form.

The most important screen button is the Submit button. When you click this, your data, as entered on the form, will be processed. So, before you press Submit, check carefully that you have completed all mandatory fields, and that what you have written is accurate.

✳ If you have made a mistake, you will be prompted to amend the data in a field (see Error messages, page 177). Sometimes, this means you have to start again!

✳ Finally, before confirming an order or a purchase, the data is usually presented onscreen and you are offered the option to confirm or change the data; see Verification on page 178.

Selecting options

Sometimes, rather than typing an answer, you need to select an option; see the example on page 172.

* If the answer to a closed question is only YES or NO, the easiest way of signalling this is to tick (or cross or check) a check box.

* For those questions that have more than two options, radio buttons may be used – you click on only one.

Error messages

If you press the Submit button and there are errors in your form, you will see an error message. Follow the instructions it gives, and all should be well!

! HANDY TIP
If you change your mind, clicking on a check box changes the entry: yes to no, or no to yes. Clicking on another radio button clears any previous click.

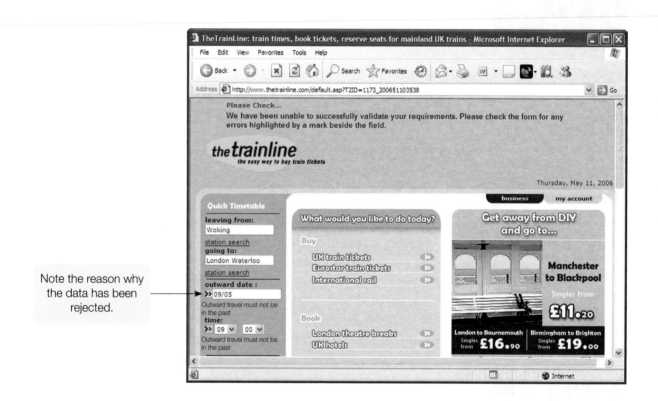

Note the reason why the data has been rejected.

YOUR TURN!

1 Return to the car insurance form. Complete all fields as accurately as possible and submit the form. Notice the different ways you can enter data: free text fields, pull-down menus, check boxes, radio buttons, etc.

2 If there is an option to clear the form, take it. Otherwise start again. This time, see what incorrect data you could enter without the system 'complaining'. What error messages are provided? How helpful are these.

Data checking

The data you enter on the form will be used for some purpose: to order some goods, to purchase a product, or to enter into a contract with an insurance company. It is therefore important that the information is accurate.

There are two processes which help to ensure that the data is as 'clean' as it can be: validation and verification.

Validation

Because the data will also affect other data already being stored on a computer somewhere, it is important that it is **valid**. For this reason, much of what you enter on a form is guided and controlled through the use of pop-up or pull-down menus, check boxes and radio buttons.

Data such as your date of birth – or the expiry date of your credit card – must be valid, so you may be guided to select a day (1–31), month (Jan–Dec) and year, all from pop-up menus. If you try to enter 30 Feb, it will be rejected!

Whenever you break one of the validation rules, an error message will appear, such as: 'The date must be a valid date.'

Verification

For much of what you enter on a form, the accuracy – or otherwise – of the facts that you enter are known only to you. The data may be valid, i.e. reasonable, and pass the validation checks, but you may be lying!

If you complete a form for an online dating agency, for example, there is no way that the computer can check whether you are truthful about your age. Nor can it check whether you really are 'blonde and petite' or 'tall, dark and handsome with good sense of humour'. So, anyone reading your details should realise that it is not necessarily true.

However, the rules of such sites usually include a condition that you will be truthful and, in pressing the Submit button, you are confirming the veracity of the content of your form. This is called the verification stage.

With transactions such as a purchase by credit card, the verification stage signals your agreement to go ahead with the purchase, so you must be very sure that you have completed the details accurately.

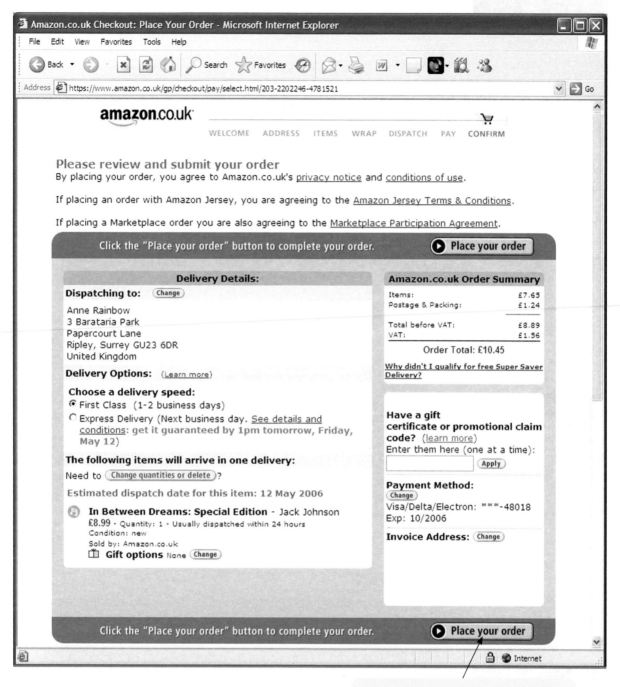

Do not click on 'Place your order' unless you have checked all the details and are sure you want to proceed.

YOUR TURN!

1 Return to the online car insurance quotation form. Look at how dates are entered. Try to enter an invalid date. What error message is displayed?

2 For a text field, experiment with entering some text, tabbing to another field and then coming back to the text field (tab on or use the mouse) and editing your text.

Taking care with personal data

In the same way that a person might not tell the whole truth when completing an Internet dating form, the person who sets up a website offering goods for sale might also not be truthful.

✻ How can you tell whether a site is genuine?

✻ How can you protect yourself from fraudulent Internet traders?

The first thing to check is the contact details. All genuine sites will include enough information for you to contact the organisation through conventional means: telephone and/or snail mail post.

You could also do a search on the name of the company or people named on the site. If there has been any scandal, a search might point you to articles of interest.

Consumer research sites offer advice on how to protect yourself.

✻ The Internet Watch Foundation website focuses on Internet abuse to do with pornographic material but also offers advice on other aspects of Internet abuse and how to protect yourself (www.iwf.org.uk).

✻ The Consumer Information site of the **FSA** offers advice on how to protect yourself from scams that arise on the Internet and elsewhere.

✻ The Office of Fair Trading (www.oft.gov.uk/consumer) offers top tips on how to avoid Internet fraud. This is of particular relevance for those who bid for goods on the Internet.

✻ eBay have a Trust & Safety team, which works to make eBay a safe and reliable place to trade.

What does it mean?

FSA
Stands for Financial Services Authority, a regulatory body which oversees accountants and insurance brokers financial dealings.

YOUR TURN!

1 The government published, as part of its UK online strategy, a paper about e-government which considers the need for authentication. Other papers address the ID card issue. Go to the Directgov portal site and use search techniques to locate relevant publications.

2 Visit the Office of Fair Trading site and read its tips. Compare notes with others in your group and share any experiences of computer fraud.

3 Visit the FSA's Consumer Information site and read the advice about protecting yourself from e-mail scams.

4 Visit the Internet Watch Foundation website and browse to discover what it does and does not cover.

5 Find out how the eBay Trust and Safety policy works.

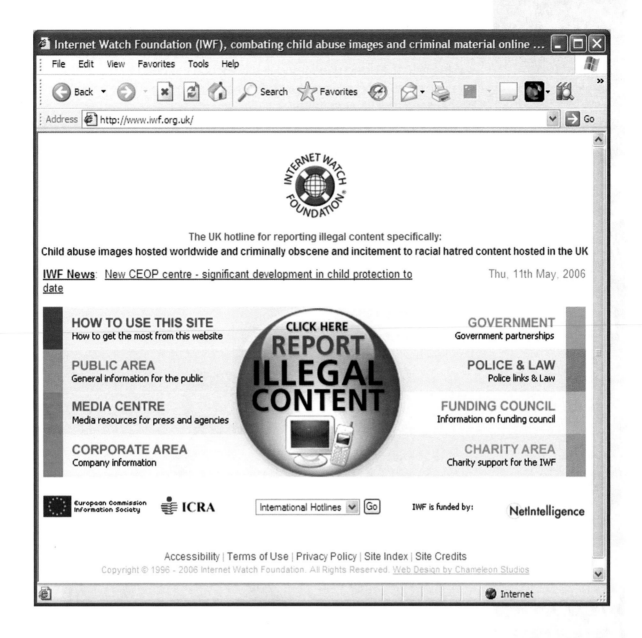

Using credit cards safely

If you plan to buy goods on the Internet, you will most likely pay for them using a credit card.

You will have to reveal some important information before the transaction can be accepted.

✳ Your credit card number is a 16-digit number which appears on the front of your card and uniquely identifies your account.

✳ The expiry date appears just beneath the credit card number. This has to be a month/year later than the current month/year; otherwise the transaction will not be accepted.

✳ You will probably also be asked to reveal the last three digits of the security number which appears on the reverse side of the card. This item of data 'proves' that you have the card in your possession.

Online services **181**

This amount of information would make it possible for anyone to buy goods and charge it to your account. So, if you lose your card, you run the risk of it being used fraudulently. Hence the need to report your card stolen as soon as you realise it has gone missing. There are other precautions that you can take.

HTTPS
See page 126.

❋ Buy only from Internet traders that you can trust.

❋ Then, when going through the payment sequence, make sure that the protocol being used is **HTTPS**.

❋ Print out details of your transactions and keep them safe.

❋ When your credit card bills arrive, check each entry. If you find an entry which you suspect to be fraudulent, contact your credit card company immediately.

The credit card companies have procedures for investigating claims of fraud. You may find that any monies charged to your account can be reimbursed, so you are not out of pocket.

YOUR TURN!

1 Look back at your credit card bills for the past three months. Do you recognise each entry as being valid?

2 Visit a site such as eBay and find out how you might be expected to pay for goods. How secure is the procedure?

3 Visit the Office of Fair Trading site and search on 'fake escrow'. Read on to find out what advice the FSA offers about your legal rights for online shopping.

Applications

In this section, you will learn how to use the services available through the Internet. You will interact with an online service provider to successfully obtain various services, and fully participate as an e-citizen in a number of areas. Nine areas are explored but, in the tests, you are only required to participate in three selected areas.

News

Newspapers, traditionally, invited comment from their readers, and printed a selection of the letters received to continue the debate on topics of the day. Some listeners and viewers would also write in to comment on radio and TV programmes. Nowadays, radio stations invite listeners to telephone in – or to write with news and views. Some television programmes also encourage listeners to call in with their points of view on topics being broadcast that day.

Instead of trying to make your views known through the telephone, you can easily e-mail the TV or radio station or newspaper. The volume of e-mails received for all such programmes allows the producers to use the 'best' comments to enrich the listening or reading experience for others in the audience.

The Internet provides an additional opportunity for members of the audience to interact with other readers and listeners via the websites run by newspapers, TV channels and radio stations.

Posting your views on the news via the Internet

The BBC website has pages set aside for each programme that it airs. For example, *The Jeremy Vine Show* is featured on www.bbc.co.uk/radio2/shows/vine/. You are invited to contact Jeremy by completing a form. If you include your telephone number – and your message is interesting enough – you might be contacted by one of the programme researchers and invited to talk on air with Jeremy.

Similarly, the editor of *The Times* invites you to join live debates online; *The Guardian* invites comments (with the tag line: Comment is free … but facts are sacred) and *The Independent* invites you to e-mail your comments.

YOUR TURN!

1 Visit the BBC site and browse to find a page that relates to a programme you listen to regularly. Check the options for contacting the programme and airing your views.

2 Access and join in with other readers on another news site, such as those provided by *The Times*, *The Guardian* or *The Independent* and look for other opportunities to make your views known.

3 Find a site for a local radio station and check what opportunities exist to join debates on local issues.

Voting on the Internet

Voting by telephone or on the Internet has become very popular. The audience participation in shows on TV like *Big Brother*, where one person is to be voted off, subject to the votes made for the more popular 'celebrities', has opened the floodgates for similar shows, and more opportunities to join in by voting on some issue of the day.

To cast your vote, you simply tick a box, or select a **radio button** as instructed. This may be cheaper than using the telephone to register your vote.

Many forum sites include polls. These can be set up by members of the site, to find out the views of other members. Writers' Dock has lots of polls; the one shown on page 186 was used to decide the venue of a get together of writers.

RADIO
BUTTON
See page 172.

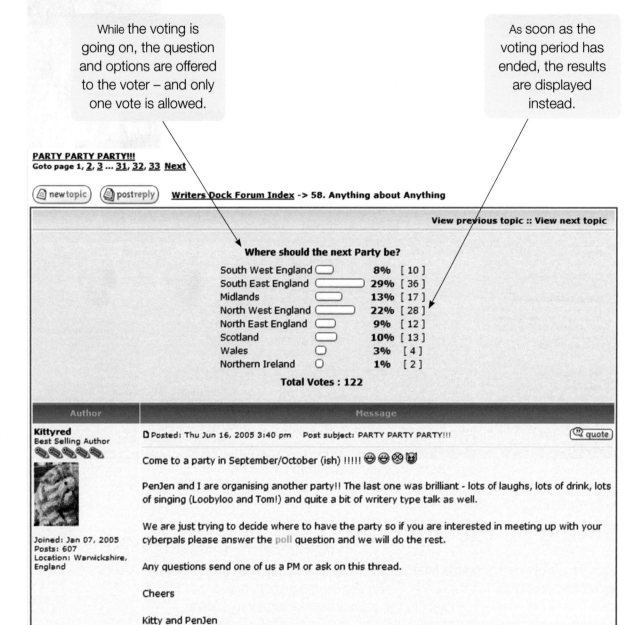

While the voting is going on, the question and options are offered to the voter – and only one vote is allowed.

As soon as the voting period has ended, the results are displayed instead.

PARTY PARTY PARTY!!!
Goto page 1, **2**, **3** ... **31**, **32**, **33** **Next**

(🖹 new topic) (🖹 postreply) **Writers Dock Forum Index** -> 58. Anything about Anything

View previous topic :: View next topic

Where should the next Party be?

South West England		8%	[10]
South East England		29%	[36]
Midlands		13%	[17]
North West England		22%	[28]
North East England		9%	[12]
Scotland		10%	[13]
Wales		3%	[4]
Northern Ireland		1%	[2]

Total Votes : 122

Author	Message
Kittyred Best Selling Author Joined: Jan 07, 2005 Posts: 607 Location: Warwickshire, England	▯ Posted: Thu Jun 16, 2005 3:40 pm Post subject: PARTY PARTY PARTY!!! (quote) Come to a party in September/October (ish) !!!!! 😃 😃 😵 😈 PenJen and I are organising another party!! The last one was brilliant - lots of laughs, lots of drink, lots of singing (Loobyloo and Tom!) and quite a bit of writery type talk as well. We are just trying to decide where to have the party so if you are interested in meeting up with your cyberpals please answer the poll question and we will do the rest. Any questions send one of us a PM or ask on this thread. Cheers Kitty and PenJen 😃

YOUR TURN!

1 Return to the BBC, and search on POLL. At the time of writing, this returned 3174 links, of which 9 of the 14 on page 1 of 318 pages relate to polls in which you could cast your vote – provided you had not missed the deadline. Select two polls of interest to you from the first few pages and cast your vote.

2 Visit your local radio station site again and check what polls they run. Cast your vote on a topic that interests you.

Government

The government has taken care to provide lots of information on its websites. Any leaflets or guidance notes are now available on the Internet.

More recently, the government has made it possible to send information to the various departments via the Internet, rather than on paper. This means it may be quicker for you, but, more importantly, the government receives the information electronically. So, it does not have the costly and time-consuming process of entering the data. Instead, we do it for them!

This section considers two examples of your providing information to the government electronically.

❄ First, you will see how you can file your tax return online. The first year this was done, the government site crashed because everyone left it to the last minute. Since then, it has run more smoothly.

❄ Then, you will see how you can register yourself for the electoral roll.

❄ Finally, you will pull together skills learned so far – browsing the Internet, and e-mail – to request information about a social services issue.

Online submission of tax returns

The personal tax year runs from 6 April one year to 5 April the next year. All individuals in the UK may be required to file a tax return, in which they declare their earnings, and to pay tax on their earnings according to rates set in the budget by the Chancellor. The hardcopy form for the return runs to many pages and, for some people, especially the self-employed, it can be a nightmare.

For those who have to file a self-assessment, the online option makes it as painless as possible.

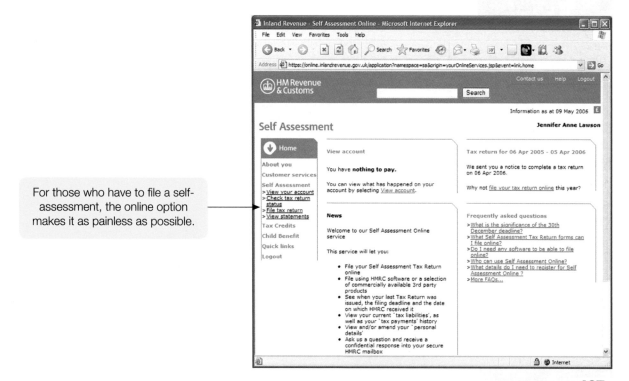

The process of filing your tax return includes the entry of the most personal data: your financial details. The system is therefore set up to protect your data from unauthorised access.

HOW TO... Register as a new user and get a user ID

1 Go to the government portal site (www.direct.gov), click on 'Do it online' and select 'File your tax online'.

2 Click on the Register button for new users.

3 Tick the check box for Self Assessment Online and click on Next.

4 The next screen, very helpfully, warns you what information you will need: your **UTR**, your **NI** number and your postcode. It also provides a link to information as to where you might find this information, and the combination of letters and numbers involved.

5 The next screen explains the process of registration, at the end of which you will be given a user ID. You then have to wait 7–10 days to receive an **activation PIN** through the post. This is to reduce fraudulent registration but delays you, so allow time for this.

6 Click Next and follow the five steps, completing the onscreen forms as instructed. Notice that an asterisk denotes a mandatory field. If you are asked to provide extra information, e.g. your e-mail address, a reason is given as to why you might reveal this information.

7 When you are asked to choose a password, notice the rules given, and that you are asked to enter it twice.

8 At step 3, be careful to enter data in the same format as per the examples. Otherwise, your entry will be rejected as invalid and you will have to enter it again.

9 At step 4, you must accept the terms and conditions before you will be allowed to use the online services. A link is provided so you can read them.

10 If what you have entered is valid, you will be issued with a user ID. If not, a polite error message will invite you to go back and check your data.

REMEMBER
A mandatory field is one that you have to complete.

! HANDY TIP
When you receive your activation code, it is only valid for a limited time.

1 Go to the HM Revenue & Customs site, and familiarise yourself with what services are provided by this site.
  If you have not already registered for online submission of your tax return, register now.
2 Government websites encourage discussion of issues. Visit www.askbristol.com and then search on issues of interest to you.
3 Political parties also have websites. Look for the site of the party you would support in the next election. Check out the sites of the other parties too.

> **! HANDY TIP**
> File your tax return before the deadline or you will incur financial penalties.

Electoral register

The electoral register is a list of the names and addresses of everyone who has registered to vote. Your local authority is required by law to make the electoral register available for viewing by anyone who asks.

Previously, anyone could buy a copy of the register, but the law has now been changed so you have some choice about who can buy your details. Nowadays, there are two versions of the register: a full version and an edited version.

When you fill in your electoral registration form, you will be asked to choose whether you wish your details to be included in the edited register.

The Electoral Commission website explains your rights but as a government agency, rather than a Whitehall department, it provides a link to the 'citizen facing' site called AboutMyVote – which invites you, as a voter, to download a registration form.

If you live in Scotland, England or Wales, then you can register to vote online, by going to www.direct.gov.uk and clicking on the DoItOnline link.

To complete the form, you will need to provide your name, your current address, a previous address where you have been registered and your date of birth.

Social services

Directgov may be your first port of call if you are looking for help through social services.

For example, if you are moving house, you may want to know if day-care services for the elderly will be available. The search engine provides a list of articles and pages that might be of interest. Following the links leads you to the information you need, and to contact details so you can ring or e-mail to register your interest.

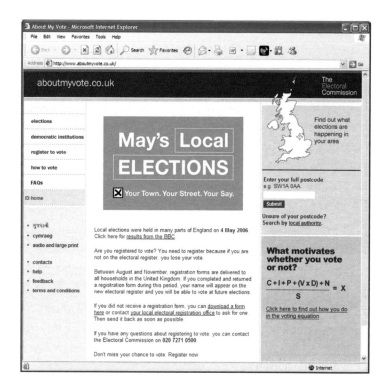

YOUR TURN!

1 Explore the AboutMyVote website and find out when your next local elections are due. If you have not already registered on the electoral roll, do so now.

2 Within your group, pool questions that you might want to ask of social services. Visit the Directgov site and look for answers to all the questions. If you cannot find the answer to a question, compose an e-mail to send to the appropriate local social services office.

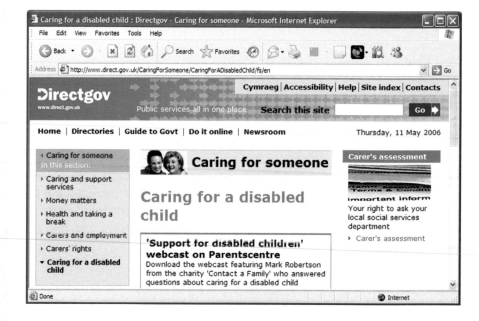

Consumer

In Block 2 (pages 141–5), you investigated online stores. You considered how you might shop online, and looked at online banking. You used the Internet to find out about entertainment and how you might book a seat and subscribe to a free newsletter so that you would be kept informed of future events. In this block, you will participate to a greater extent by taking on the role of Internet consumer:

* You could send an e-mail to your bank asking about online banking. You could transfer money between accounts, or pay a bill.
* You could purchase a theatre ticket, a CD or a book.
* You could obtain a quotation for a car purchase.
* You could join a consumer watchdog group or subscribe to a consumer newsletter.

The tasks you decide to do will reflect your own circumstances and your personal preferences.

Bank transfers

The option to transfer money between accounts online gives you power over your money. You should keep only minimal amounts in your current account to meet cheques, standing orders and direct debits – and earn interest on any unneeded amounts by keeping them in higher interest accounts.

Transferring money between your current account at a bank and a savings account at a building society still takes a few days – this is a quirk of the banking system! However, if you want to transfer monies between accounts held at the same bank then this is done instantly. So, it makes sense to have a savings account with your bank – and to use that to make the best use of spare monies.

The process of transferring money is straightforward and your bank's website will take you through it, step by step.

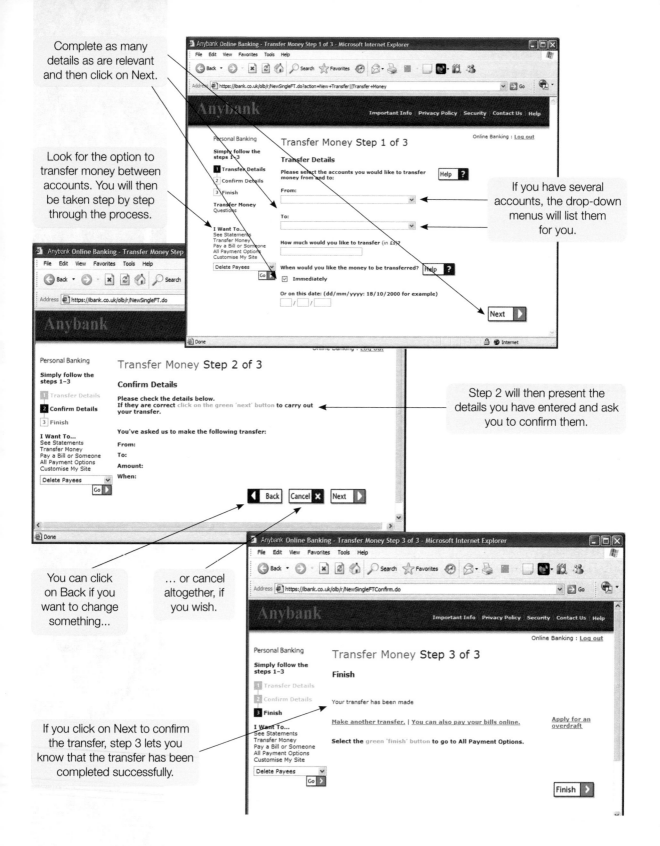

Complete as many details as are relevant and then click on Next.

Look for the option to transfer money between accounts. You will then be taken step by step through the process.

If you have several accounts, the drop-down menus will list them for you.

Step 2 will then present the details you have entered and ask you to confirm them.

You can click on Back if you want to change something...

... or cancel altogether, if you wish.

If you click on Next to confirm the transfer, step 3 lets you know that the transfer has been completed successfully.

YOUR TURN!

1 Find out how to transfer money between accounts for your bank.

2 Investigate interest rates available on savings accounts, and how long it takes to transfer money between your various accounts.

Online stores

There are many sites that offer goods such as CDs and books. Amazon.com is one of the most well-known online retailers of books, CDs, videos, DVDs and so on. However, there are now many others for you to choose from.

Most online stores let you track recent orders, view your account and change your order if you want to.

Purchasing goods and services online

Imagine you want to buy a book or CD online – and decide to shop with Amazon. Amazon has many departments and provides a search tool for you to find exactly what you want. Amazon also offers links to sections with gift ideas, new releases, top sellers (updated hourly!) and today's deals.

Having located the book or CD you want to buy – through searching and/ or browsing – add it to your **shopping basket** by clicking on the 'Add to shopping basket' icon.

You can then continue to browse the site, adding more items to your shopping basket if you wish.

Many online stores tell you what items they think might interest you. They list items that people with the same taste as you (who bought what you have chosen) have bought. This may introduce you to new writers or artists; the intention is to encourage you to buy more items.

What does it mean?

SHOPPING BASKET
This icon is used to signify a file which lists purchases made during a visit to an online store.

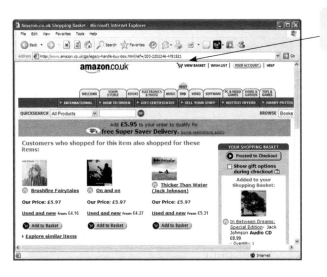

Shopping basket icon

YOUR TURN!

1 Go to an online store's website, like Amazon, and follow the process of buying a book or CD. You can opt out of the actual purchase at the very last confirmation stage if you really don't want to buy.

2 Explore the items that the site suggests might suit you. What data must the site retain to be able to provide this information for you?

Obtaining quotations

Buying a small-priced item on the Internet is easy, convenient and relatively risk free. If you wanted to buy a much higher-priced item, though, you might use the Internet to obtain a quotation from a number of potential vendors before making a decision.

For example, you might want to buy a new computer system from an organisation such as Dell, or a new car.

Before the organisation can give you a quotation, you have to specify what you want, and this will involve completing a form and making some selections.

If the quotation is too high (or too low!), you have the option to amend your requirements. The quotation will then be recalculated.

At each stage (type, engine, budget), make choices using the drop-down menus.

YOUR TURN!

1 Go to an online store's website, like Dell, and follow the process of obtaining a quotation for a laptop. Print out the quotation.

2 Browse to find the website of the manufacturer of your car, or one that you might like to own. Make choices on the number of doors required, and extras such as a sunroof or air conditioning, then obtain a quotation for your ideal car. Amend your choices and compare prices.

A night out!

The Internet is an ideal source of information about entertainment opportunities.

✳ Many cinema complexes advertise their programmes on websites.

✳ Most theatres have their own sites with information of the plays that may be seen during the forthcoming season, together with articles on the actors.

Because these venues would like a full house, there are often some last-minute offers for cheaper seats.

Sites like Lastminute.com pull together information about good deals, not only for theatres but also for flights, hotels, holidays, hotel accommodation, car hire and gift ideas.

YOUR TURN!

1 You have already bookmarked the site of your local theatre or cinema complex (Your Turn!, page 145). Return to the site, and book two seats for a show during the next month. Fill in the credit card form but do not complete the transaction (unless you want to).

2 You remember that a friend has a special anniversary this week and has expressed an interest in a visit to an opera. Search the lastminute.com site to see what is available in the next few days.

> **! HANDY TIP**
> Many sports clubs have excellent online booking facilities. Check out the website of any sports sides you support.

Subscribing to newsletters

You could make a point of visiting sites of interest to you, to see what's new. However, a more efficient way of keeping up to date with developments is to subscribe to a consumer newsletter.

In the Your Turn! on page 145, you visited the London for Fun website and considered subscribing to any newsletter offered. You only need to supply an e-mail address and you will be included in the bulk e-mailing of a newsletter. As soon as you subscribe, you will receive a 'thank you' e-mail which reads: 'You have successfully subscribed to the London cultural events and exhibitions newsletter. Thank you. Team London for Fun.'

If you decide, having seen the newsletter, that you would rather not receive it any more, there has to be an opt-out provided by the publisher of the newsletter. Exactly how to unsubscribe varies from publication to publication, so you need to follow the instructions provided.

If you subscribe to a newsletter, you will receive regular e-mails. The first one may go to your Bulk e-mail inbox. If so, tell the spam filter that it is not spam.

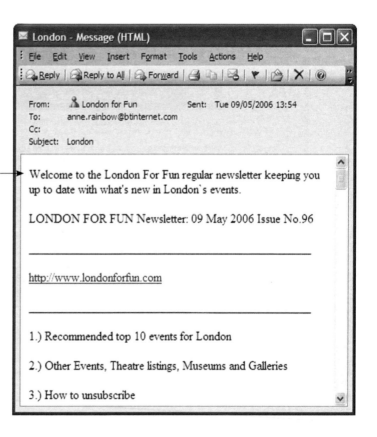

YOUR TURN!

1 Subscribe to a newsletter that you think you might like to receive, by entering your e-mail address.

2 As per instructions received via the bulk e-mailing of this subscription newsletter, unsubscribe from the service.

Consumer watchdog groups

The National Consumer Federation (NCF) encourages and co-ordinates the work of voluntary, independent local consumer groups, individual consumers and those who have an interest in consumer affairs through other organisations; it represents their views nationally.

Local consumer groups investigate a wide range of issues of concern to local people in their communities. They campaign to seek improvements in local services and facilities, such as shopping, transport, healthcare, recreational, and even public conveniences! The group members volunteer their time and pay subscriptions for the general good. All consumer groups publish a regular newsletter for their members, and this is a good way of learning more about what they do.

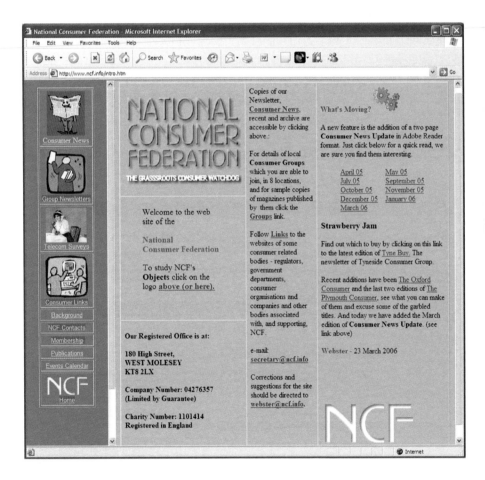

YOUR TURN!

1 Search the NCF site for information on how you might join a group local to you, and download a newsletter for such a group.

2 Visit www.consumerdirect.gov.uk to find out what this site has to offer.

Travel

In Block 2 (pages 146–9), you used the Internet to make travel plans: by air to Australia, including a stopover; and to a European capital.

You also looked at train and coach services to your nearest airport, and to an event such as a sports tournament. You explored sites that provided accommodation, both overseas and in the UK.

In this block, the focus is on travel by car, but the activities extend the investigative work that you did in Block 2, so that you experience the process of booking a flight, arranging hotel accommodation and buying a train ticket.

Booking a flight

The Internet provides access to powerful search engines which can find just the right flight for you. There are several websites offering this service; search on 'cheap flights' and select from one of those offered.

You will need to provide details of your proposed journey, and then the search engine will offer you the results: lots of flights with different airlines. Decide which flight you want to take. You will then be led through a series of screens to pay for the flight and make other choices like food preferences and where you would like to sit in the aircraft. You may also be offered links to sites that offer accommodation and car hire.

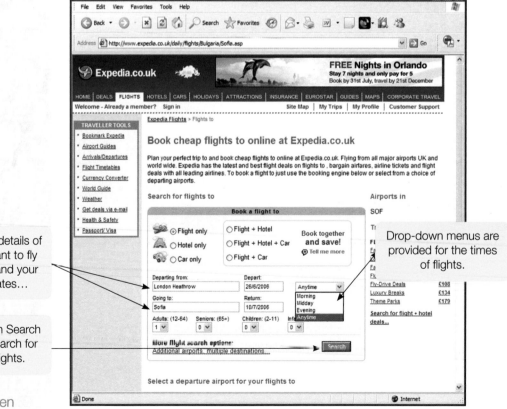

Complete the details of where you want to fly from and to, and your preferred dates...

... and click on Search to start the search for matching flights.

Drop-down menus are provided for the times of flights.

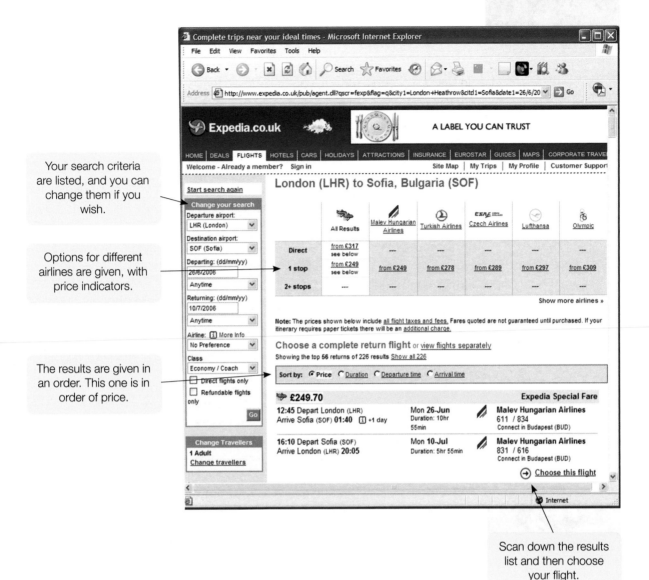

Your search criteria are listed, and you can change them if you wish.

Options for different airlines are given, with price indicators.

The results are given in an order. This one is in order of price.

Scan down the results list and then choose your flight.

YOUR TURN!

1 For one of your travel plans, book your flight. If you have the option, select a seat and your choice of in-flight meal.

2 For another of your travel plans, book a hotel room. Check that the room suits your needs (no smoking, bath/shower, etc.).

Travel by car

You have visited the Multimap website before and will be aware of the option to plan a route from one place to another. There are many other sites which offer this facility.

The AA (Automobile Association) site is also a treasure trove of information for motorists. The AA's main 'product' is its breakdown cover, so this features prominently on their site.

However, they offer insurance cover too, not only for your car, but also for your home and travel; and they offer loans, which might help you to buy a new car.

Their route planner gives a choice of route, e.g. avoiding motorways and toll roads. The route planner results tell you how far you will travel and gives an estimate for the time of the journey. It offers SMS traffic alerts so that you can receive – as text messages on your mobile phone – advance notice of congestion, accidents and road works, before you set out and during your journey.

Similar sites exist for other motoring organisations, e.g. the RAC (Royal Automobile Club) and Green Flag.

YOUR TURN!

1 Visit the site of one of the motoring organisations. Check out the features available on the site.
    Compare this with what is offered by one of the rival organisations.
2 Visit the UpMyStreet website (www.upmystreet.com) to look for information on the location of petrol stations on the route from your home to the nearest airport.

> **! HANDY TIP**
> Some travel sites invite you to comment on your trip. You might use the views of other travellers to help you to decide where to stay.

3 Search the AA/RAC/Green Flag sites for what options you have to break your journey and stay in a B&B hotel.
4 For another of your travel plans, buy a train ticket online. Use a site, such as Trainline, to work out what time you will need to leave your house to catch the train.

Education/Training

In Block 2 (pages 150–4), you located adult education courses in your neighbourhood. You also looked at e-learning opportunities, and the facilities available on library sites.

In this section, you will extend these activities by, for example, enrolling for a night class, sending an e-mail requesting information about a course, and reserving a library book online. You will also participate in an interactive Internet classroom or course environment.

Enrolling on a course

In the Your Turn! on page 150, you identified courses for yourself and a neighbour. To book on one of these courses, you will need to complete an enrolment form, and pay for the course online using your credit card.

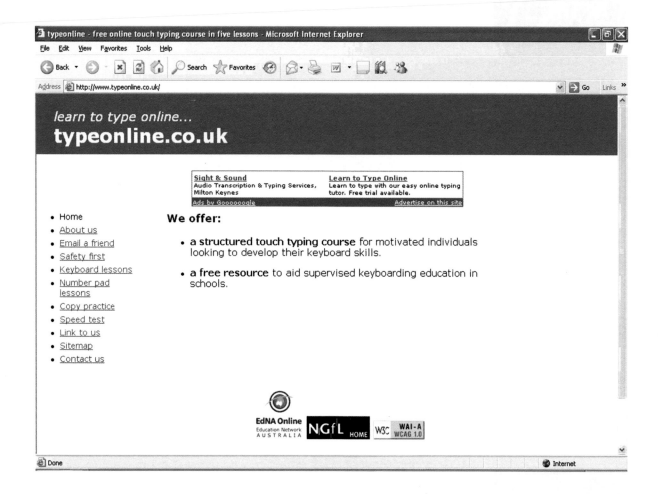

YOUR TURN!

1 Locate the site for a free online course of your choice. Enrol for the course, completing an enrolment form.

2 Bookmark any other courses that interest you, but that are not free.

Making enquiries

Sometimes, you need more information than a website provides before you can make a decision about a course.

❋ Do you have the necessary skills or previous knowledge to benefit from this level of course?

❋ What exactly does it cover?

You could telephone the college or council who are responsible for running the course, but this may be inconvenient if the opening times do not match when you are free to call them. Or it may be expensive, e.g. if you only have a mobile phone or are abroad.

Instead, you could e-mail your enquiry. Most sites provide contact details and, often, these include an automatic link to an e-mail address. If you click this link, it opens up your e-mail software, and completes the To field for you.

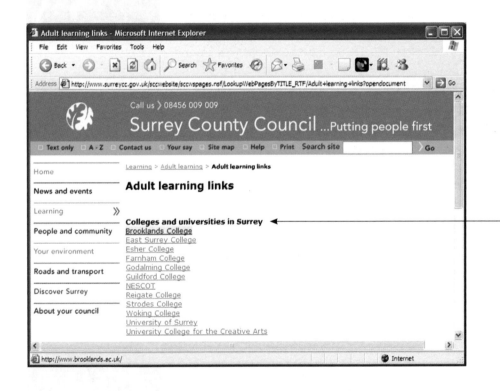

Locating your nearest college is easy. Clicking on a link opens the website for that college, and all the contact information is then available to you.

YOUR TURN!

1 Go to the site that gives details of a course you might want to join. Bookmark this site if you haven't done so already. Browse to find an e-mail link, then click on it.

2 Complete the e-mail, requesting some additional information, and send it.

3 Look in your Sent folder, and add the contact details to your Address Book.

Making reservations

In Block 2 (pages 153–4), you located the website for your local library and checked that your personal details were correct. In this block, you will extend this activity by making reservations. (You must be a member of the library; if you are not already, this will involve a visit to your library. Take with you proof of your residency in the borough, e.g. your driving licence and/or a recent utility bill.)

In this section, you will consider two different types of reservation:

* You will learn how to reserve a book. There is no standard layout for library sites, so you may have to search the catalogue to find the details of the book, and then opt to reserve it if such a link is offered. Or there may be a direct link to reserving books from the library home page.

* You will learn how to reserve a timeslot on a computer at the library. More and more libraries offer this service: a boon for people without their own computers, who are perhaps relying on Internet access at work.

Because the sites differ, you need to 'read' each page of your local library site to find what you are looking for. Remember that most sites offer a search facility, and many also provide a **site map**. Either of these may help you to track down what you want.

You will need to enter your library card number and PIN number before you can carry out any transactions that affect your personal account. This is a normal safety precaution.

You will also have to complete forms during the process of making a reservation.

! HANDY TIP
For the web address of your local library, look on your library card.

What does it mean?

SITE MAP
This list of hyperlinks shows the structure of a site, so you can see exactly what is on offer.

HOW TO... Reserve a book online

 1 Locate the details of the book by searching the catalogue.

 2 Select the 'Reserve this book' option by clicking on the screen button.

 3 Complete additional information as requested, e.g. your library number and PIN number.

 4 Some libraries charge a fee for making reservations. Check that you are happy with the terms and conditions of the reservation before confirming your request to reserve the book.

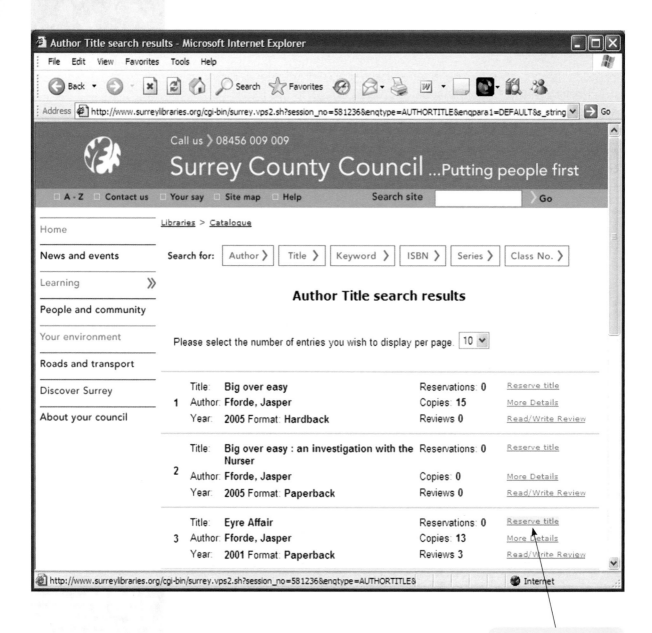

Locate the book you want to reserve, using the Search option in the catalogue. Then click on Reserve title.

YOUR TURN!

1 Find out what books might be useful for a course that you have enrolled on. You might have to send an e-mail to find out the answer to this question.

2 Locate these books in the library catalogue, and reserve one of them for your personal use.

Reserve a PC online

 1 Log on to your library site by entering your library number and PIN number.

 2 Locate and select the option to reserve a PC.

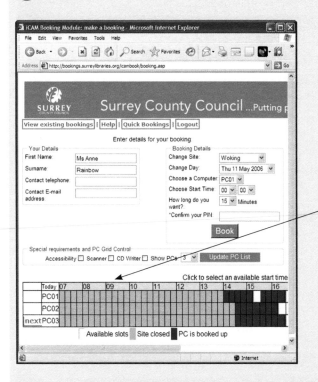

You can check the availability of PCs before you try to make a booking.

 3 A new window may open. Check that your details are correct, and then start completing the booking details part of the form. There may be more than one site and at each one there will be a number of PCs available. Select the venue that is most suitable for you.

 4 Complete the day by selecting a date from the drop-down menu.

 5 Refer to the availability section of the form, and click on the start time that suits you. This may automatically complete the 'Start time' field on the form.

 6 Using the drop-down menu, complete the number of minutes you require. Note: there may be a limit as to how long you can book for any one session.

 7 You may need to confirm your PIN before clicking on the Book button.

8 If the computer (or venue) that you chose is booked up already, choose a different PC, or a different location. As a last resort, choose a different day.

> **REMEMBER**
> Clicking on the downward arrow will reveal a drop-down menu.

9 Having made the booking, the next screen confirms the details.

 10 If you change your mind, you ought to cancel the booking and free up that time slot for another person.

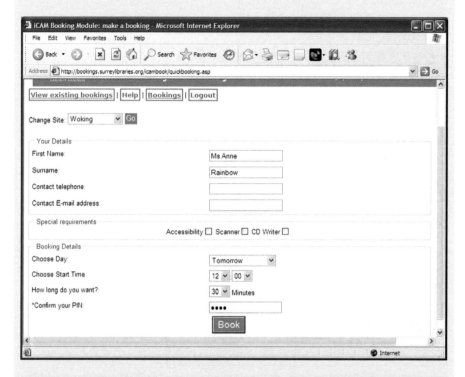

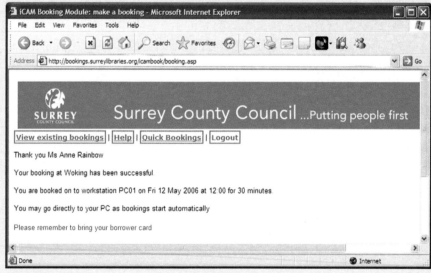

YOUR TURN!

1 Go to your library site and complete a booking to use one of the PCs for two hours.

2 Cancel your booking.

Employment

In Block 2 (pages 154-9), you investigated the availability of information about job vacancies on the Internet.

You learnt about how you might prepare the data for a job application form, and may have practised completing one.

In this block, you will extend this activity, and create your **CV** to e-mail to a prospective employer or recruitment agency. You will send your CV to an online recruitment agency, and apply for a job. You will also e-mail for details.

Writing a CV

A CV describes you and your life to date: your history of work and education, and any details that may encourage a prospective employer to offer you a job interview.

You could handwrite your CV, but if you plan to send it electronically, it makes sense to create it using word processing software. A word-processed CV may also look more professional.

There are lots of websites offering advice as to what to include in your CV and how to lay it out.

* If you search *Google*, with the keywords 'Writing CV', a number of sites will be listed which have been created by students as part of a course in website development (or something similar). They are 'amateur' sites but still offer sound advice.

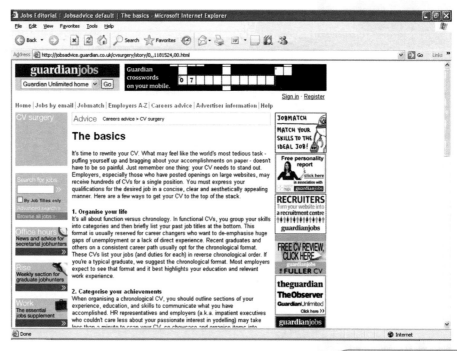

* Some sites offer a 'professional' CV writing service. This means you will be asked to pay for the service!

* The DfES government site offers free advice, and a PDF that you can download.

* The Jobcentre also offers assistance on its site: www.jobcentreplus.gov.uk.

You should never lie on your CV. However, depending on the job you are applying for, you may want to omit some information and expand on other aspects of your history. It helps, therefore, to have one CV which lists everything – all your qualifications and your past jobs – and from this you can tailor a CV for a particular job application.

> **REMEMBER**
> A PDF is a type of file that can be read using *Adobe Acrobat Reader*.

REMEMBER
Use File Save As to save a file with a changed name, one that shows it is the newest version. See page 60.

YOUR TURN!

1 Refer to two or three websites that offer advice as to how you might present your CV.

2 Collect together any details that you might need to create or revise your CV.

3 Open a word processing document and create your CV. Preview it on screen and, when you think you are happy with it, print it out. Ask friends or family to look at it and suggest any changes.

4 Amend your CV, saving it with a name that indicates the version number and/or the date you modified it.

Recruitment agencies

A recruitment agency acts as a go-between, between job seekers and employers with job vacancies.

The recruitment agency charges the prospective employer a fee for any successful placement, but makes no charge to prospective employees. However, their objective is to earn their fee and so their loyalty, if any, lies with the employer.

The introduction of websites for recruitment agencies makes it even easier for them to build up a list of prospective employees. It is in their interest to have as many people as possible 'on their books' and they will encourage you to register, even if there are no jobs that suit you at the moment. However, you have nothing to lose in registering.

A search on the Internet using the keywords 'recruitment agency' gives a long list of agencies. Perhaps it would be better, though, to refine your search so that you include the county where you live, and/or the city where you would like to work. You should then be able to find an agency that is near you or where you want to work, and the job location is more likely to be where you want it.

HOW TO... **Sign on to an agency**

 1 Choose an agency. Look them up in your local telephone book, or search for one on the Internet.

 2 Some agencies, such as www.totaljobs.com, offer a search by location. You may also have the option to specify a distance from a particular location.

A hit list of jobs will be presented to you. For any that appeal to you, click on the link offered to view further details about the vacancy.

Some recruitment agencies, such as RecruitmentExpress, offer a 'Forward my details' option. This includes an email link, so an email is set up automatically for you to send your CV as an attachment for a particular vacancy.

Having found a job, if you click on 'Forward my details' an e-mail opens up automatically, to which you could attach your CV.

The To and Subject fields are set up for you automatically.

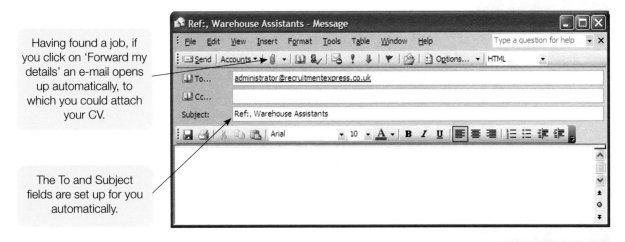

YOUR TURN!

In this activity, the focus is on 'receptionist' vacancies. If you wish, replace the keyword 'receptionist' with one which is more relevant for you.

1 Search the Internet to find a recruitment agency that specialises in jobs for receptionists and other administrative staff.

2 Complete an online form to register your interest in any vacancies for the post of receptionist.

> **REMEMBER**
> You can practise your IT skills without completing the process. Click Reset rather than Submit if you do not want to register.

Health

In Block 2 (pages 159–61), you looked at the WWW as a source of information about health and, in particular, alternative medicines and private healthcare.

In this block, you will practise your e-mailing skills in contacting health service agencies for information.

❋ You could e-mail your optician or dentist (or other health clinic) to book an appointment for treatment.

❋ You could e-mail your doctor to ask for information about vaccinations that you might need for a forthcoming holiday.

You will also look at what is involved in filing an insurance claim.

Feet, eyes and teeth

To keep yourself feeling good, you may need regular treatments, e.g. a visit to your chiropodist, an eye test or a dental check. If you are already registered with a practitioner, you may have booked your next appointment the last time you went. But if you need to change this, or to request a new appointment, you could telephone, or it may be more convenient to send an e-mail.

YOUR TURN!

1 Use the Internet, or other sources, to find the e-mail addresses for any health practitioners that you need. Add these addresses to your e-mail address book.

2 Send an e-mail to one of your practitioners, requesting an appointment, or changing an appointment that you have already made. Make sure you include enough information: your full name and any reference numbers that would identify you.

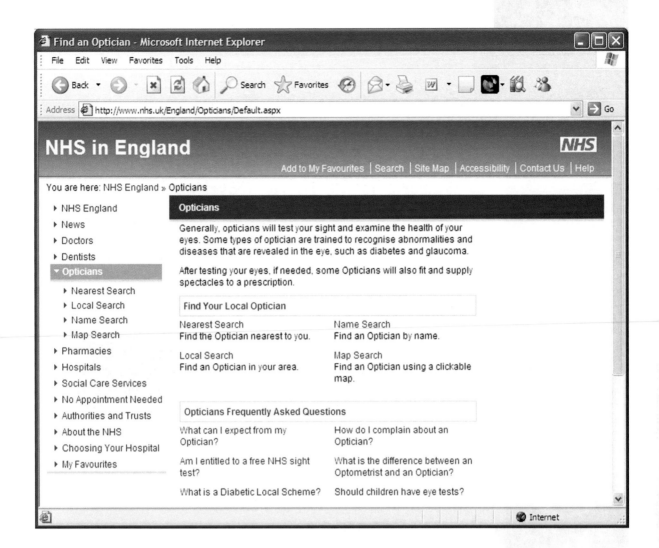

Vaccinations

If you plan to travel abroad, for some places you are advised to have vaccinations prior to travel.

The WWW can be a useful source of this information. For example, compiled and updated by a team of experts from the Travel Medicine Division at Health Protection Scotland (HPS), the NHS website www.fitfortravel.nhs.uk offers travel health information.

Having identified what you think you may need, you might need to arrange to have the injections in a particular time period. This is because some vaccinations take time to give protection.

Say that you need to have them 4–8 weeks before you travel. You could ring your doctor's surgery for an appointment, but if staff are busy taking calls from people trying to book appointments that day, an e-mail may be a more effective way of contacting your GP.

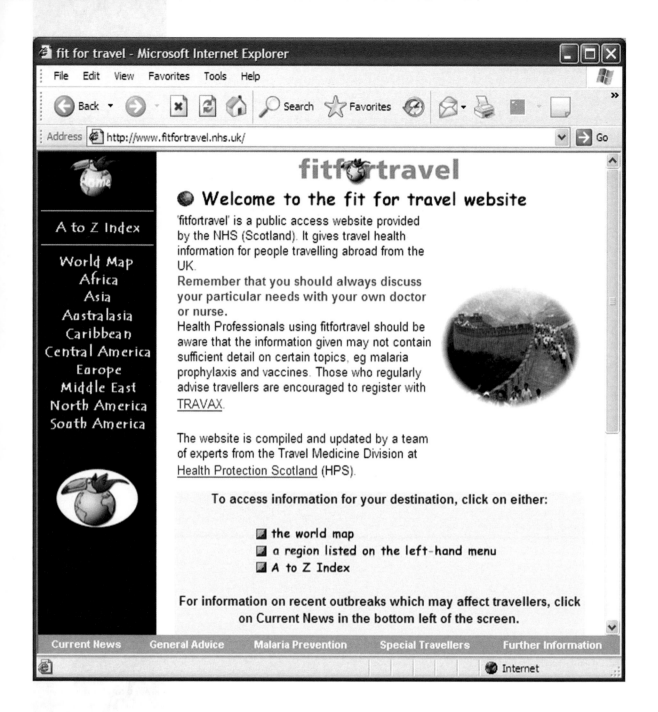

YOUR TURN!

1 Search the WWW for sources of information on vaccinations recommended to travellers.
What diseases are you at risk from catching if you travel overseas?

2 Visit the NHS site www.fitfortravel.nhs.uk – or another similar site – and find out what vaccinations are needed to travel to a place that you might want to visit. Bookmark any sites of interest.

3 Compose an e-mail to send to your doctor to request confirmation of the vaccinations that you will need, and to ask for an appointment within the relevant period prior to such a visit overseas.

Making an insurance claim

Before you can make a claim against your own insurance, you normally need to have paid premiums for whatever level of cover you think necessary. The other option is to claim damages against someone else's insurance.

Whenever you travel, you ought to have arranged your own travel insurance, which should at least fund your return to the UK in the event of some disaster. The travel company through whom you book a holiday is quite likely to offer insurance, but this may not be the most cost-effective option for you. And if you are a frequent traveller, you might be advised to obtain cover for a whole year rather than for each trip.

There is an increasing inclination among people to claim damages for injuries – and there are organisations keen to represent you, with the promise of no win, no fee.

If you decide to make an insurance claim, whichever route you take and whoever's insurance company has to pay, there will be a form to complete, and this may be available online.

> **! HANDY TIP**
> A holiday that seems too good to be true may not be such a good deal when you add up all the extras, including travel insurance.
> So it pays to look around to find the best deal.

YOUR TURN!

1 Investigate the costs of travel insurance cover for a fortnight's holiday in a destination of your choice. What does it cover? What is excluded?

2 Investigate the options to claim damages following a traffic accident, or stumbling while out walking.
Visit sites such as Start2Claim (www.start2claim.com) and check what you would have to do to make a claim.

3 Visit the site of your own insurance company and check what is included for public liability insurance (which is how someone might claim against you).

Interest groups

In Block 2 (pages 164–6), you looked at community groups, voluntary groups and online discussion groups. You investigated these groups and located some in your neighbourhood. In the Your Turn! on page 164, you were prompted to join the writers' website *Writers' Dock* and to post a message.

In this block, you will extend this to take a more active role in these groups, online.

Joining an online discussion group

It is important that you choose a group of interest to you, and have the time to join in with discussions. It is also important not to let the discussion group take over your life!

Let's suppose that you want to join an online book review group. Guardian Unlimited runs such a group on their website (http://books. guardian.co.uk/bookclub). It offers you the 'chance to read and discuss books with other book lovers' and provides the facility for you to discuss one book a month. They choose the next month's title when the discussion starts, thus giving you plenty of time to read up for the next session.

You don't have to register to read what others have said, but you do need to register if you want to post a message yourself on the talk boards.

HOW TO... **Register for Guardian Unlimited reading group**

> **! HANDY TIP**
> Notice that the UK is at the top of the list of countries.

1 Go to the Talk area of the *Guardian Unlimited* site. Click on 'Start talking'. Notice that you are a 'guest'. Before you can chat, you must click on 'Sign in'.

2 A new window opens. Click on the text link 'Click here to register for the first time'.

3 Complete the registration form.

4 Click on the 'Click to register' button.

When you first register, as a security measure, Guardian Unlimited sends you an e-mail confirming your registration.

Similarly, if you alter your details, you should receive an e-mail confirming your account.

As soon as you have confirmed your registration, then you can post comments.

One extra facility offered on Guardian Unlimited – which tends to be offered on other sites with 'talk' or chat rooms – is that you can choose a name by which you want to be known. So long as no one else has already chosen that name, it is assigned to you, and no one need know your real identity. The same goes for anyone you 'talk' to. They may have the name 'Jane' but actually be called 'Jim'!

> **! HANDY TIP**
> If you don't receive a confirmation e-mail immediately, check that you spelt your e-mail address correctly! Check also that it has not been put in your Bulk inbox by your spam filter software.

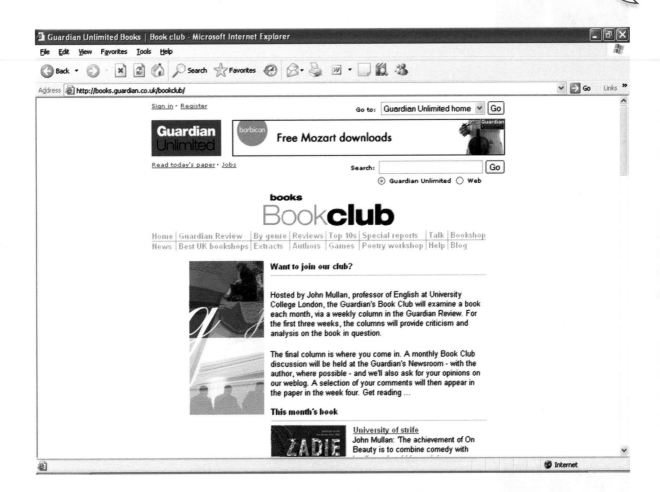

YOUR TURN!

1 Investigate the WWW for discussion groups of interest to you.

2 Register with one group. Be careful to enter your e-mail address correctly. Choose a password that you can remember but is not too easy for others to guess. Confirm your registration when you receive the confirmation e-mail. Read some of the threads on the site and post a message.

Business

In Block 2 (pages 161–4), you spent some time searching for organisations in your neighbourhood. You also looked at intranets and extranets.

This section focuses on company intranets.

By definition, access to a company intranet is normally limited to employees of the company, so you should not be able to access the intranet of any other organisation. For this reason, the images shown here are from Heinemann's intranet.

One use of an intranet is internal communication.

* Employees can contact each other through an internal e-mail system. This can be used to let each other know when and where a meeting or a training session is due to take place.

* The intranet can be a source of information for all employees, and the posting of such information will fall to individual contributors. For example, a sales manager may be responsible for publishing the previous month's sales figures, and announcing the winner of the salesman of the quarter award.

* The intranet can be used for electronic communications to replace hardcopy-based systems. For example, employees may be encouraged to report faults by completing an online form which is then automatically sent to the facilities manager for action.
  As another example, expense claims could be completed online, and be based on a spreadsheet form so that all the arithmetic is done automatically. At the close-off date, these forms could be submitted to the Finance Department for processing.

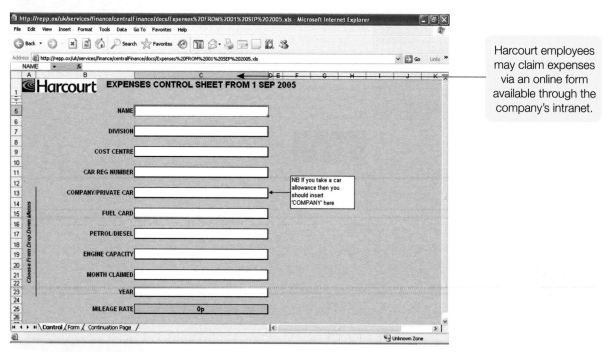

Harcourt employees may claim expenses via an online form available through the company's intranet.

Some organisations may also allow a bulletin board facility so that employees can post messages for all to see. This facility might be used to announce some leisure event that everyone is invited to attend, e.g. a leaving party. It might also be used to advertise possessions for private sale, such as a car.

YOUR TURN!

1 If your company has an intranet, and there is an option to submit an expense claim online, explain to others in the group how this is done. Be careful not to disclose any confidential information.

2 If your job entails writing reports, such as sales reports, and you are expected to post these reports to the company intranet, explain how you do this to others in your group.

3 If your company intranet allows posting of messages, explain how this works to others in the group.

Record of achievement

Tick the boxes as you work through this course. When you have ticked everything you should be ready to take the examination.

BLOCK 3: e-Participation

	Done	Revised
ONLINE SERVICES		
What is an online form?	☐	☐
How online forms work	☐	☐
Data checking	☐	☐
Taking care with personal data	☐	☐
Using credit cards safely	☐	☐
APPLICATIONS		
News	☐	☐
Government	☐	☐
Consumer	☐	☐
Travel	☐	☐
Education/Training	☐	☐
Employment	☐	☐
Health	☐	☐
Interest groups	☐	☐
Business	☐	☐

Glossary

Activation PIN	A number that gives a user access the first time they use a secure site.
Applications	The programs that are on your computer, like Word and Excel.
Arrow keys	Keys that let you jump up and down a line, or back and forth one character.
ATM	Automated teller machine.
Backspace key	A key on the keyboard; deletes the character before the cursor.
Backup	Copy of a file kept for security reasons.
BCC	Blind carbon copy (of an e-mail).
Blogging	Revealing personal information through a private web page as in a journal or diary.
Bookmark	A URL remembered in your Favorites folder.
Boot sector	A special area on a disk, used to hold data needed when starting up a computer.
Broadband	A fast connection between computers along telephone lines.
Browse	To click your way through your directory structure, until you find a particular file or folder.
Browser	Software that gets pages from the WWW and displays them on your screen.
Brute force attack	A hacker trying all possible passwords until one allows access to the account.
Bulk mailing	The same e-mail message sent to many recipients.
Caps Lock key	A key on the keyboard; when on, a character appears in capitals.
CC	Carbon copy (of an e-mail).

Clip Art	Images that are available, maybe free of charge, that you can use to jazz up your document.
Clipboard	A temporary place for things when you cut or copy them.
Cloaking	Hiding behind some disguise (as used by viruses).
Crash	When the computer screen freezes and clicking the mouse or pressing keys on the keyboard has no effect.
Cursor arrow	A key on the keyboard; allows movement of the cursor up a line, down a line, back a character and forward a character.
CV	Curriculum vitae.
Deep linking	Linking to a particular page within a site, rather than the home page.
Default	A setting that is decided by the software vendor, but one that you can change if you want.
Delete key	A key on the keyboard; deletes the character after the cursor.
Desktop	Like a real life desktop, what you see onscreen: your documents and tools such as a clock and a calculator.
Directional keys	Keys that let you jump up and down a page, or to the beginning or end.
Directory	Pre-Windows name for a folder – where files are stored.
Distribution list	The e-mail addresses of people to whom you might need to send the same e-mail message.
Drag and drop	A way of moving material; click on the object and hold the button down while dragging the object to a new position on the screen. When the button is released the object is 'dropped' into position.
E-book	A novel or other 'book' that is published in electronic form rather than (or as well) as in hard copy form.
E-learning	Using materials that are published on the WWW for self study.

E-mail	Short for electronic mail.
Enter key	A key on the keyboard used to start a new line, or to complete the entry of data.
Favorites	A folder in which to store all bookmarks, i.e. links to websites you may want to revisit.
Field	The place for a single item of data.
File extension	A 3- or 4-character code that appears after the dot in a filename.
Flash	Software needed for some animations to work onscreen.
Flash BIOS	An area in the computer memory, used to hold data essential for starting up a computer.
Font	A particular shape of lettering of which there are two main types: sans serif (without 'feet', e.g. Arial) or serif (with 'feet', e.g. Times Roman).
Form	A screen full of data fields laid out for easy completion so as to collect data from the user.
FSA	Financial Services Authority.
Function keys	The 12 keys along the top of the keyboard.
FYI	For your information.
Hard copy	A printout on paper, rather than on the screen or on a disk.
Hard drive	A storage device.
Hit list	A list of websites that match some criteria, including a hyperlink to each site.
Hot keys	Combinations of keys that, when pressed together, have a special effect, such as a function key with the Shift key or Ctrl or Alt.
Hotlink	An image or some text that, when clicked, takes you to a different web page or place within a document.
Housekeeping	Keeping the storage space tidy, often by deleting unwanted files and folders.

HTML	Hypertext mark-up language.
HTTP	Hypertext transfer protocol.
HTTPS protocol	Similar to HTTP but using a different port for a more secure link.
Hypermedia	Data in a variety of formats: text, sound, graphical images and animation.
Identity fraud/theft	Using another person's personal details, such as credit card information, to purchase goods and services fraudulently.
Inbox	Where incoming e-mails arrive.
Intranet	An internal, closed network with access restricted to members of a group.
IP	Internet protocol.
IRC	Internet relay chat.
ISP	Internet service provider.
Junk mail	Unsolicited mail.
Keyboard	An input device used to enter text and commands.
Keyword	A word (or phrase) used by the search engine to identify websites whose content match it.
Landscape	Orientation with the longer side along the top.
Logical drive	A disk drive is given a logical drive letter: A and B for floppy disks, C for the hard drive, D for a CD, etc.
Mandatory	Compulsory.

Menu	A list of commands, which lead to submenus of more commands.
Modem	A hardware device that modulates and demodulates a computer signal.
Monitor	An output device.
Mouse	A pointing device used to move the cursor and to make commands.
NI	National Insurance.
Object	A single item, such as a window, a text box, or an image.
Online help	Guidance about an application, built into the software or available over the Internet.
OPEN	Olympic and Paralympic Employment Network.
Outbox	Store for outgoing e-mail messages.
Password	A secret string of characters (letters and digits) used to gain access to private data or programs.
PDF	Portable document format.
Peripheral	An input or output device that is attached to a computer, e.g. mouse, keyboard, printer.
PIN	Personal identification number.
Point size	The vertical height of a font.
Port	Part of the computer which enables you to connect to extra devices; an entry (or departure) point for data – and maybe hackers and viruses.
Portrait	Orientation with the shorter side along the top.
Processor	The part of the computer that controls all other parts – its 'brain'.
Protocol	An agreed set of rules.

Reboot	Close down and restart.
Recycle Bin	A place to put files you no longer want; they stay in the Recycle Bin – and you can get them back – until you empty the Recycle Bin, and then the files are no longer available.
Rescue disk	Emergency disk containing enough software to restart your PC, plus antivirus software so that you can clean an infected PC.
Roll over	The cursor can be moved over an object, e.g. to reveal what it does or is.
Scroll bar	An indicator at the side and/or bottom of the window that can be dragged to reveal more of the display.
Search engine	A research tool used to find websites that meet given criteria.
Search key	The keywords needed to find what you are looking for.
Shift key	A key on the keyboard; it provides an extra meaning to each key. For letters, it turns lower case into upper case (and vice versa if Caps Lock key is on). For numbers, it gives other characters like ! " £ $ …
Shopping basket	An icon used to signify a file which lists your purchases during a visit to the online store.
Shortcut	A key combination or a mouse button that jumps you to an option.
Site map	A list of hyperlinks showing the structure of a site.
Snail mail	Affectionate term for the postal delivery system used for 'normal' mail; so named because it is so slow when compared to e-mail.
Spam	Another name for junk mail.
Spamming	E-mailing or making the same comment repeatedly or across different groups.
Spell checker	A software tool that compares words in a document with those in an electronically stored dictionary.
Sponsored links	Websites that have paid to be included in the hit list for certain keywords.

Tab order	The order in which the fields are to be entered (on a form).
Text editor	Software that offers simple but very limited features to create a text file.
Thread	A string of comments (or tiles) forming a conversation between the members of a group.
Toggle	To switch between two states by pressing the same button.
Toolbar	A grouped selection of icons, e.g. of formatting commands.
URL	Uniform resource locator.
USB	Universal serial bus; a fast connector for peripherals such as modems, mice and external storage devices.
UTR	Unique taxpayer reference.
Valid	Reasonable, that is within an expected range, the right length or the right type or format of data.
Virus	A program that can cause damage to the data on a computer.
Virus protection software	Software that attempts to trap viruses and therefore prevent them from damaging data and software.
Virus signature	A feature of a virus that identifies it.
Webmail	E-mail services available via the Internet, such as a Hotmail account.
Window	A rectangular area through which you view your workspace.
Word processing package	Sophisticated software that offers more text editing features than a basic text editor.

Wordwrap	Formatting option which automatically puts text on to a new line when a line is filled.
WWW	World Wide Web.
Zoom in	To magnify an image in order to show more detail.

Index

Note: Page numbers in bold refer to definitions of key terms.